# Chords & Scales
# for Guitar

## by Blake Neely and Jeff Schroedl

Speed • Pitch • Balance • Loop

To access audio visit:
**www.halleonard.com/mylibrary**

Enter Code
3236-1117-1379-5765

ISBN 978-0-7935-7417-9

Visit Hal Leonard Online at
**www.halleonard.com**

Contact Us:
**Hal Leonard**
7777 West Bluemound Road
Milwaukee, WI 53213
Email: info@halleonard.com

In Europe contact:
**Hal Leonard Europe Limited**
42 Wigmore Street
Marylebone, London, W1U 2RN
Email: info@halleonardeurope.com

In Australia contact:
**Hal Leonard Australia Pty. Ltd.**
4 Lentara Court
Cheltenham, Victoria, 3192 Australia
Email: info@halleonard.com.au

# INTRODUCTION

Hello again. We say "again" because we're assuming that you've already been through **FastTrack Guitar 1** and **2**. (At the very least, **Book 1**.) If so—terrific! You've decided to keep learning your instrument and you're ready for this supplemental book.

This book provides five important things:

 Basic guitar chord theory

 Easy-find index of over 1,400 different guitar chords and voicings

 Basic scale and mode theory

 Patterns for 8 scales and 7 modes

 Special "Jam Session" using the chords and scales introduced

> IMPORTANT: This book is a reference book (much like a dictionary) and should not take the place of a guitar instruction book. That being said, please go through **FastTrack Guitar 1** and **2** before starting this book.

Remember, if your fingers hurt, take a break. Some of these chords and scales require some serious stretching. With practice and patience, you can learn them all (and avoid cramping).

So, when you're ready, tune up, crack your knuckles, and let's learn some chords and scales...

# ABOUT THE AUDIO

Glad you noticed the added bonus—audio! Each of the tracks in the special "Jam Session" are included, so you can hear how it sounds and play along. Take a listen whenever you see this symbol:

# WHERE TO FIND THINGS

**PRIMER**    4

What's a chord?    4
Table of chord suffixes    4
Building chords    5
Table of intervals    5
Everything's relative    6
Building to scale    7
Choosing the best voicing    8
Fingerboard diagrams    9

**CHORDS**    11

| | | |
|---|---|---|
| no suffix | major | 12 |
| m, min, − | minor | 13 |
| +, aug, (♯5) | augmented | 14 |
| sus4, sus | suspended fourth | 15 |
| (add9) | added ninth | 16 |
| m(add9) | minor added ninth | 17 |
| 5, (no3) | fifth | 18 |
| 6 | sixth | 19 |
| m6, -6 | minor sixth | 20 |
| 6/9 | sixth, added ninth | 21 |
| m6/9 | minor sixth, added ninth | 22 |
| 7, dom7 | seventh | 23 |
| °7, dim7, dim | diminished seventh | 24 |
| 7sus4, 7sus | seventh, suspended fourth | 25 |
| maj7, M7 | major seventh | 26 |
| m7, min7, -7 | minor seventh | 27 |
| m(maj7) | minor, major seventh | 28 |
| maj7(♭5) | major seventh, flat fifth | 29 |
| m7(♭5) | minor seventh, flat fifth | 30 |
| +7, 7(♯5) | augmented seventh | 31 |
| 7(♭5) | seventh, flat fifth | 32 |
| 7(♭9) | seventh, flat ninth | 33 |
| 7(♯9) | seventh, sharp ninth | 34 |
| +7(♭9) | augmented seventh, flat ninth | 35 |
| 9 | ninth | 36 |
| maj9, M9 | major ninth | 37 |
| m9, min9 | minor ninth | 38 |
| 11 | eleventh | 39 |
| m11, min11 | minor eleventh | 40 |
| 13 | thirteenth | 41 |

**SCALES**    43

Explanation of patterns    44
Caged system    45
Three-Notes-Per-String system    45
Horizontal system    45
Moveable Patterns    46
Guitar Fretboard Chart    47
Major scale    48
Minor scale    49
Harmonic minor scale    50
Melodic minor scale    51
Minor pentatonic scale    52
Major pentatonic scale    53
Blues scale    54
Diminished scale    55

**MODES**    56, 57

**JAM SESSION**    59

Heavenly Ballad    60
Medium Rock    60
Wall of Fame    60
Wild and Crazy    60
Full Deck Shuffle    61
Generic Pop    61
Funky Feeling    61
Don't Stop    61
Smooth Jazz    61
Overtime    61
Nashville Dreamin'    62
Heavy Rock    62
Alley Cat    62
Fusion    62
South of the Border    62
Scare Us    63
Swing It!    63
Metal Mix    63
Rock 'n' Roll    63
Outta Here    63

# LET'S DIVE RIGHT IN

## What's a chord?

A chord is defined as three or more notes played at the same time. Chords provide the **harmony** that supports the melody of a song.

Sometimes chords are indicated by **chord symbols**, written (usually) above the musical staff. A chord symbol is simply an abbreviation for the name of that chord. For example, the symbol for an **F-sharp minor seven** chord would be **F♯m7**.

## Get organized...

A chord symbol tells us two things about the chord—**root** and **type**:

1. The **root** gives the chord its name. For example, the root of a C chord is the note C. However, the root note is not always at the bottom of the chord. Notice the difference in these two types of C chords:

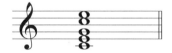　　　　

　　　　C major with C on bottom　　　　C minor with G on bottom

2. The chord's **type** is indicated by a **suffix** (m, 7, sus, maj9). There are lots of chord types and suffixes, but there's no need to panic—with a little practice, they're easy to recognize. This book groups all the chords by their type, so keep this list handy:

| Suffix | Chord Type | Suffix | Chord Type |
|---|---|---|---|
| no suffix | major | m7, min7, -7 | minor seventh |
| m, min, - | minor | m(maj7), m(+7) | minor, major seventh |
| +, aug, (♯5) | augmented | maj7(♭5), maj7(-5) | major seventh, flat fifth |
| sus4, sus | suspended fourth | m7(♭5), m7(-5) | minor seventh, flat fifth |
| (add9) | added ninth | +7, 7(♯5) | augmented seventh |
| m(add9) | minor added ninth | 7(♭5), 7(-5) | seventh, flat fifth |
| 5, (no3) | fifth (a.k.a. "power chord") | 7(♭9), 7(-9) | seventh, flat ninth |
| 6 | sixth | 7(♯9), 7♯9 | seventh, sharp ninth |
| m6, -6 | minor sixth | +7(♭9) | augmented seventh, flat ninth |
| 6/9 | sixth, added ninth | 9 | ninth |
| m6/9 | minor sixth, added ninth | maj9, M9 | major ninth |
| 7, dom7 | seventh | m9, min9 | minor ninth |
| °7, dim7, dim | diminished seventh | 11 | eleventh |
| 7sus4, 7sus | seventh, suspended fourth | m11, min11 | minor eleventh |
| maj7, M7 | major seventh | 13 | thirteenth |

Of course, you may run across other types of chords from time to time, but the ones listed above are the most common.

# BUILDING CHORDS

Chords are built from simple "building blocks" called **intervals**. An interval is the distance between any two notes. Here's a look at the basic intervals, using C as a root:

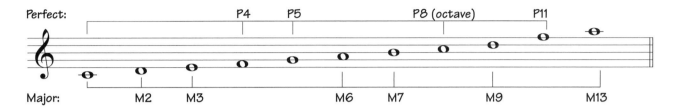

Notice that these intervals are divided into two groups—**major (M)** and **perfect (P)**. EASY TO REMEMBER: 4ths, 5ths, octaves and 11ths are perfect; all other intervals are major.

## Everything's relative...

Intervals come in many shapes and sizes, but in only five categories: **major, minor, perfect, augmented** and **diminished.**

Here's how the categories are related:

A **major** interval lowered
one half step equals a **minor** interval.

A **major** or **perfect** interval raised
one half step equals an **augmented** interval.

A **perfect** interval lowered
one half step equals a **diminished** interval.

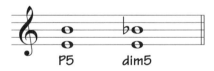

An interval's **type** is determined by the number of **steps** between the two notes.

 HELPFUL REMINDER: On your guitar, from one fret to the next equals one half step; two frets apart equals one whole step.

Review the following chart and get to know all of the interval types...

| Interval | Abbreviation | Steps | Pitches | Interval | Abbreviation | Steps | Pitches |
|----------|--------------|-------|---------|----------|--------------|-------|---------|
| unison | unis | none | | major sixth | M6 | 4 1/2 | |
| minor second | m2 | half | | augmented sixth* | aug6 | 5 | |
| major second | M2 | whole | | minor seventh* | m7 | 5 | |
| augmented second* | aug2 | 1 1/2 | | major seventh | M7 | 5 1/2 | |
| minor third * | m3 | 1 1/2 | | perfect octave | P8 | 6 | |
| major third | M3 | 2 | | minor ninth | m9 | 6 1/2 | |
| perfect fourth | P4 | 2 1/2 | | major ninth | M9 | 7 | |
| augmented fourth* | aug4 | 3 | | augmented ninth | aug9 | 7 1/2 | |
| diminished fifth* | dim5 | 3 | | perfect eleventh | P11 | 8 1/2 | |
| perfect fifth | P5 | 3 1/2 | | augmented eleventh | aug11 | 9 | |
| augmented fifth* | aug5 | 4 | | minor thirteenth | m13 | 10 | |
| minor sixth* | m6 | 4 | | major thirteenth | M13 | 10 1/2 | |

* NOTE: As with sharps and flats, some intervals may sound the same but be written two ways (for example, aug4 and dim5). Notes or intervals that sound the same but are written differently are called **enharmonic equivalents**.

## One step further...

Building chords is easy—simply add intervals to the root. The type of intervals used determines the resulting chord type. Let's start by learning some basic three-note chords built on a C root:

**Major** chords contain a
M3 and a P5 on the root.

**Minor** chords contain a
m3 and a P5 on the root.

Once you're familiar with basic chord types,
tons of other chords can be built simply by adding, subtracting, augmenting, or diminishing intervals.

# BUILDING TO SCALE

The notes of a chord can also be determined by assigning a numeric **formula**, indicating the tones used from the major scale. For example, based on the C major scale, 1-♭3-5 would mean play the root (C), a flatted third (E♭), and the fifth (G)—a C minor chord!

The chart below is a construction summary of the chord types in this book (based on the key of C only):

C MAJOR SCALE = C-D-E-F-G-A-B-C

(1 2 3 4 5 6 7 1)

| Chord type | Formula | Note names | Chord names |
|---|---|---|---|
| major | 1-3-5 | C-E-G | C |
| minor | 1-♭3-5 | C-E♭-G | Cm |
| augmented | 1-3-♯5 | C-E-G♯ | C+ |
| suspended fourth | 1-4-5 | C-F-G | Csus4 |
| added ninth | 1-3-5-9 | C-E-G-D | Cadd9 |
| minor added ninth | 1-♭3-5-9 | C-E♭-G-D | Cm(add9) |
| fifth | 1-5 | C-G | C5 |
| sixth | 1-3-5-6 | C-E-G-A | C6 |
| minor sixth | 1-♭3-5-6 | C-E♭-G-A | Cm6 |
| sixth, added ninth | 1-3-5-6-9 | C-E-G-A-D | C6/9 |
| minor sixth, added ninth | 1-♭3-5-6-9 | C-E♭-G-A-D | Cm6/9 |
| seventh | 1-3-5-♭7 | C-E-G-B♭ | C7 |
| diminished seventh | 1-♭3-♭5-♭♭7 | C-E♭-G♭-B♭♭ | C°7 |
| seventh, suspended fourth | 1-4-5-♭7 | C-F-G-B♭ | C7sus4 |
| major seventh | 1-3-5-7 | C-E-G-B | Cmaj7 |
| minor seventh | 1-♭3-5-♭7 | C-E♭-G-B♭ | Cm7 |
| minor, major seventh | 1-♭3-5-7 | C-E♭-G-B | Cm(maj7) |
| major seventh, flat fifth | 1-3-♭5-7 | C-E-G♭-B | Cmaj7(♭5) |
| minor seventh, flat fifth | 1-♭3-♭5-♭7 | C-E♭-G♭-B♭ | Cm7(♭5) |
| augmented seventh | 1-3-♯5-♭7 | C-E-G♯-B♭ | C+7 |
| seventh, flat fifth | 1-3-♭5-♭7 | C-E-G♭-B♭ | C7(♭5) |
| seventh, flat ninth | 1-3-5-♭7-♭9 | C-E-G-B♭-D♭ | C7(♭9) |
| seventh, sharp ninth | 1-3-5-♭7-♯9 | C-E-G-B♭-D♯ | C7(♯9) |
| augmented seventh, flat ninth | 1-3-♯5-♭7-♭9 | C-E-G♯-B♭-D♭ | C+7(♭9) |
| ninth | 1-3-5-♭7-9 | C-E-G-B♭-D | C9 |
| major ninth | 1-3-5-7-9 | C-E-G-B-D | Cmaj9 |
| minor ninth | 1-♭3-5-♭7-9 | C-E♭-G-B♭-D | Cm9 |
| eleventh | 1-3-5-♭7-9-11 | C-E-G-B♭-D-F | C11 |
| minor eleventh | 1-♭3-5-♭7-9-11 | C-E♭-G-B♭-D-F | Cm11 |
| thirteenth | 1-3-5-♭7-9-11-13 | C-E-G-B♭-D-F-A | C13 |

 NOTE: Since the guitar has only six strings, certain notes must sometimes be left out. And sometimes certain other notes are "doubled" (played twice). In general, the fifth and root are the first two pitches omitted when necessary.

# CHOOSING THE BEST VOICING

**E**ach chord can have several different **voicings.** A voicing is the same chord but with a rearrangement of the notes (which means you'll also have to rearrange your hand and finger position). For each individual chord, this book gives you **four** voicings to choose from…you're welcome!

Although (in theory) you may use any of the four voicings in any situation, each group does suggest a specialized function. A chord's location, difficulty, size, and intended musical style all contribute to this determination. Here's how each of the four voicings were chosen and how they should be used:

## Voicing #1

The top diagram is the most common **upper position** voicing. It's also the most appropriate for strumming purposes.

## Voicing #2

This diagram always gives you a convenient "all-purpose" voicing, usable in almost any musical setting.

## Voicing #3

Here you'll find another good "all-purpose" voicing. However, this voicing is often a **broken set** form, which means that the chord contains a lower bass note and two or three notes on higher strings with at least one "interior" string omitted. It works best in jazz or blues styles as a nice **comping** (another word for "accompanying") chord.

 NOTE: Not all of the third voicings are shown as broken chords. For those that are, though, pluck them with your fingers (rather than the pick) and simulate a piano-type sound. Be sure to "mute" the omitted strings.

## Voicing #4

**Closed** voicings (or **adjacent set** chords) are used for the fourth group. These often appear "up the neck" and work great for jazz, blues and rock styles. Due to the lack of a lower bass note, these voicings produce a thinner, less-full sound. But this isn't (necessarily) bad, especially when playing with another guitarist or as a complement to the bass player.

**PRACTICE TIP:** Don't get too bogged down with all this "theory" stuff. Just look up the chords you need and learn to play them. Heck, make up your own chords—if it sounds good, play it! If you come across a chord type not listed in this book (and you will eventually), either build the chord with the intervals named in the suffix, or reduce it to a more common seventh or ninth chord.

## Just in case...

Here's a reminder of how to read the new markings on the fingerboard diagrams in this book:

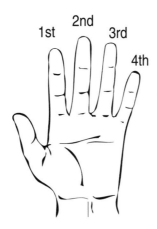

Think of your left-hand fingers as being numbered 1 through 4

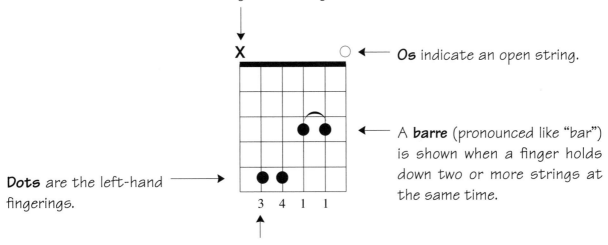

**Xs** above the grid tell you to avoid strumming that string.

**Os** indicate an open string.

A **barre** (pronounced like "bar") is shown when a finger holds down two or more strings at the same time.

**Dots** are the left-hand fingerings.

**Numbers** below the strings tell you which finger to use on that string.

NOTE: **Fret numbers** ("5fr") may appear to the right of the first fret on some chord diagrams. This tells you to slide your hand up to the appropriate fret, position your fingers and strum away. If no fret number is shown (or you see a thick top line on the diagram), your hand should be around fret 1, near the **nut.**

# ORDS

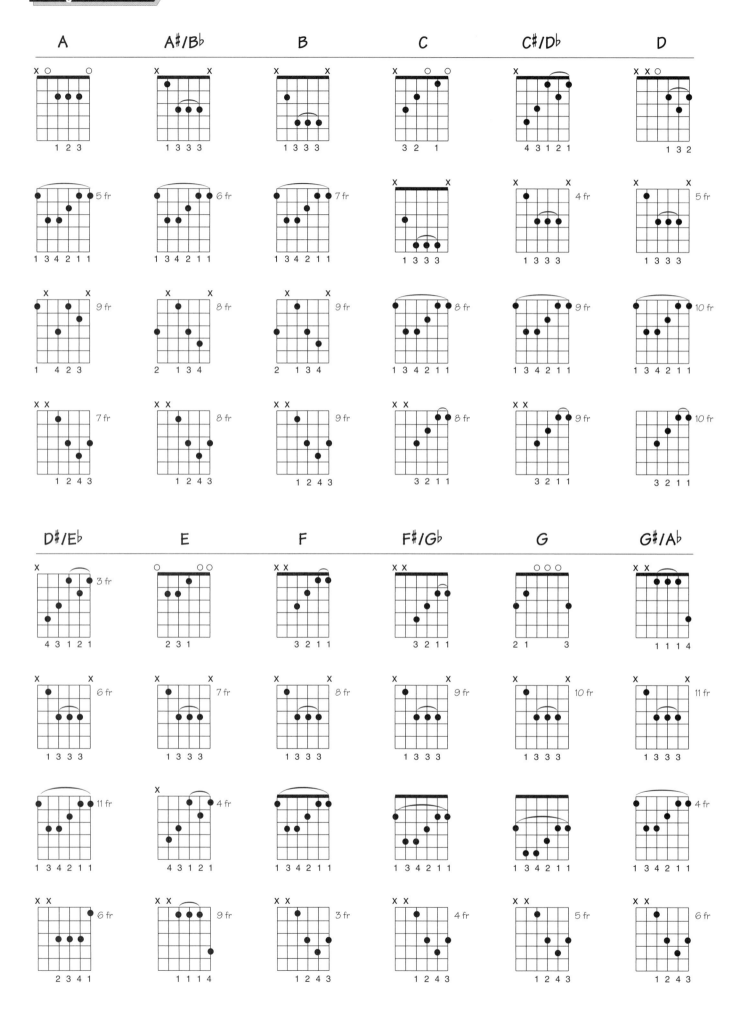

# Minor

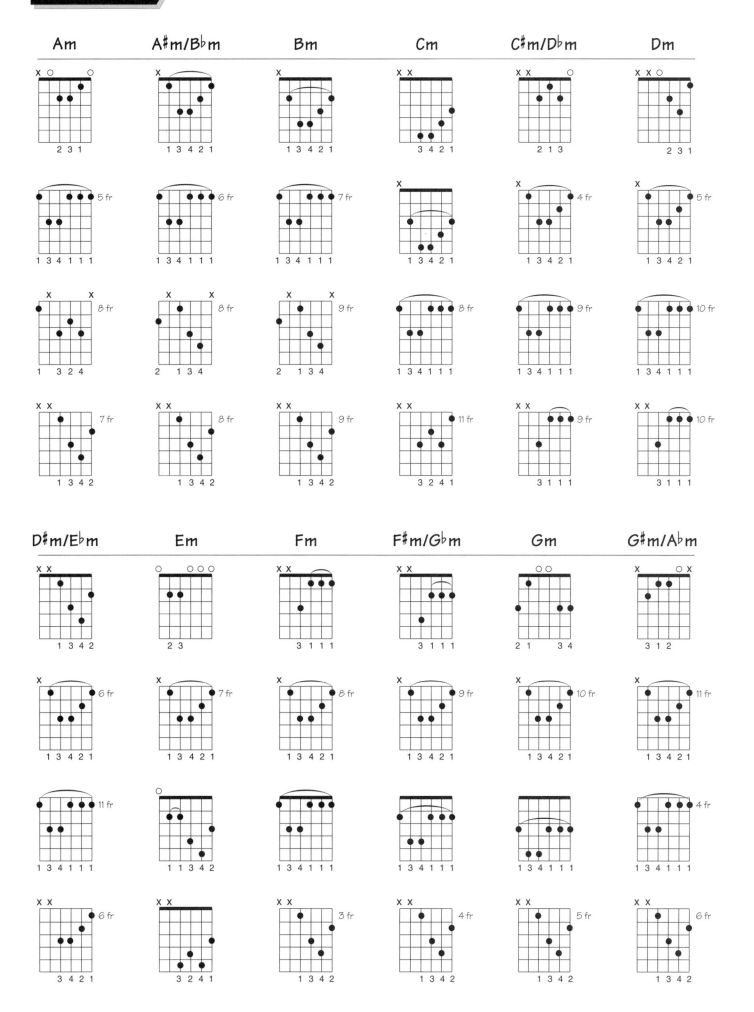

# Augmented

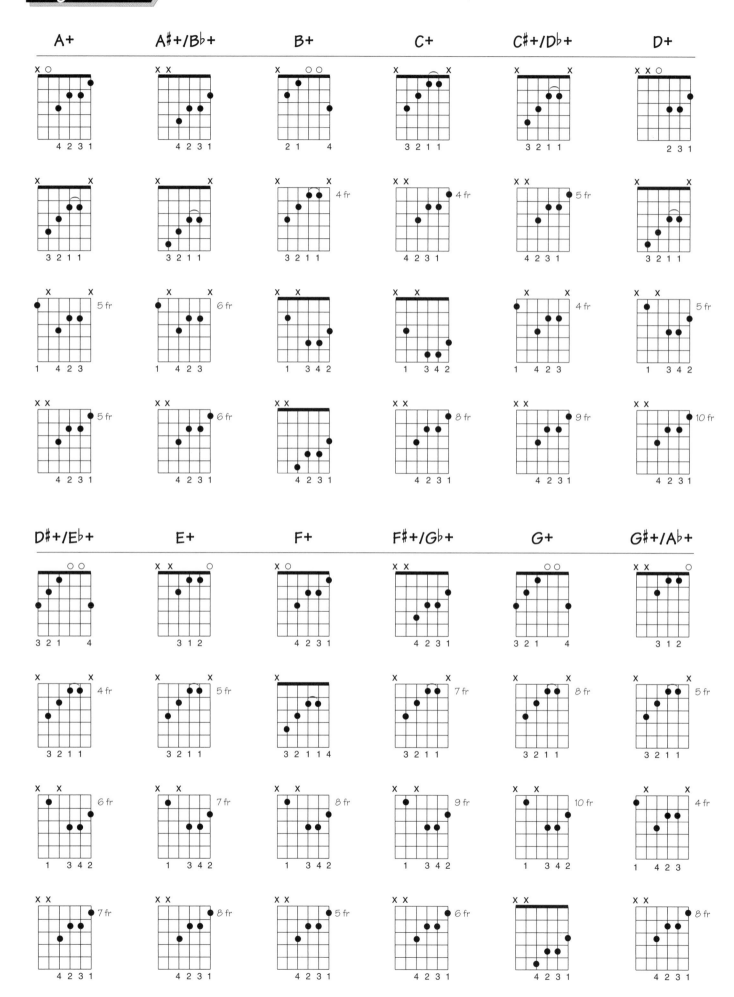

# Suspended Fourth

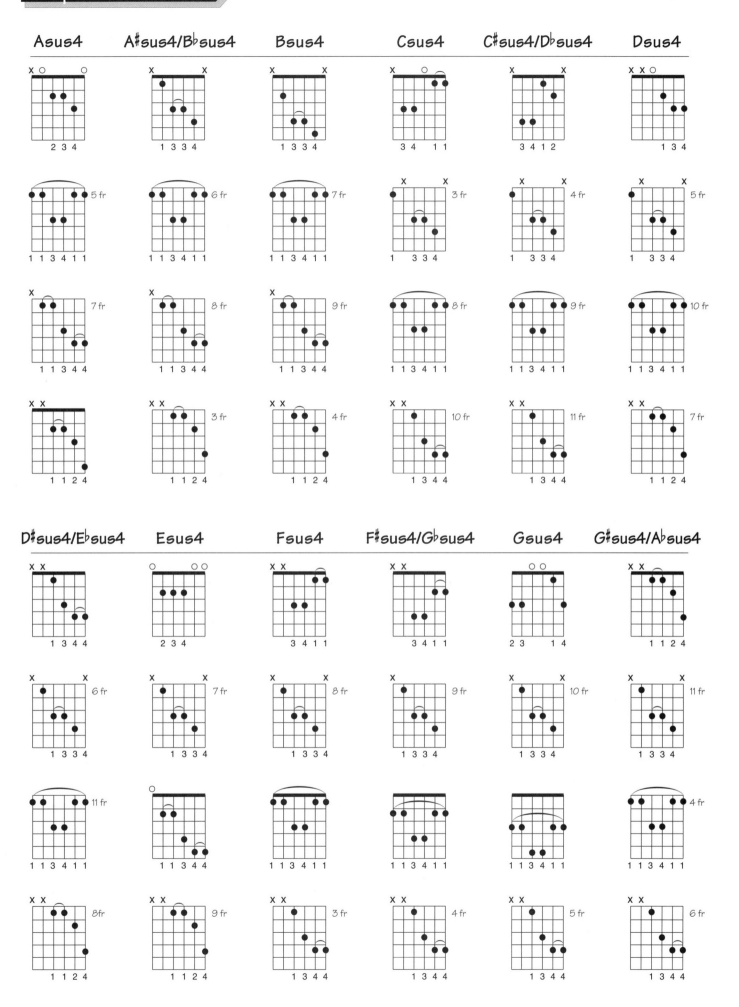

Asus4  A#sus4/Bbsus4  Bsus4  Csus4  C#sus4/Dbsus4  Dsus4

D#sus4/Ebsus4  Esus4  Fsus4  F#sus4/Gbsus4  Gsus4  G#sus4/Absus4

## Added Ninth

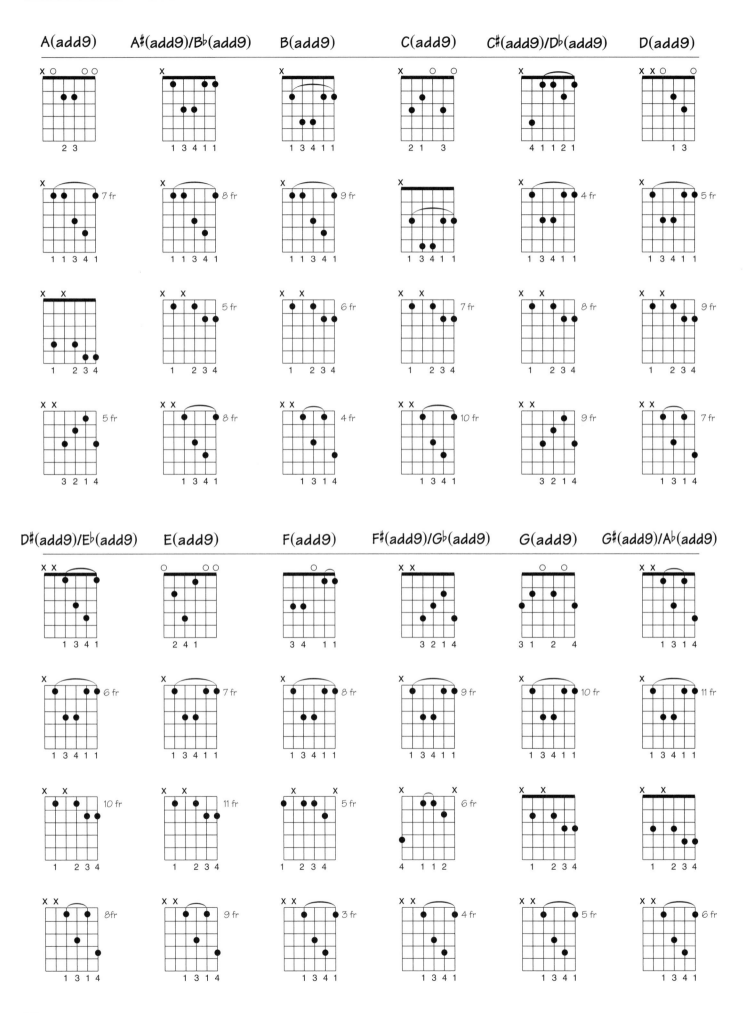

# Minor Added Ninth

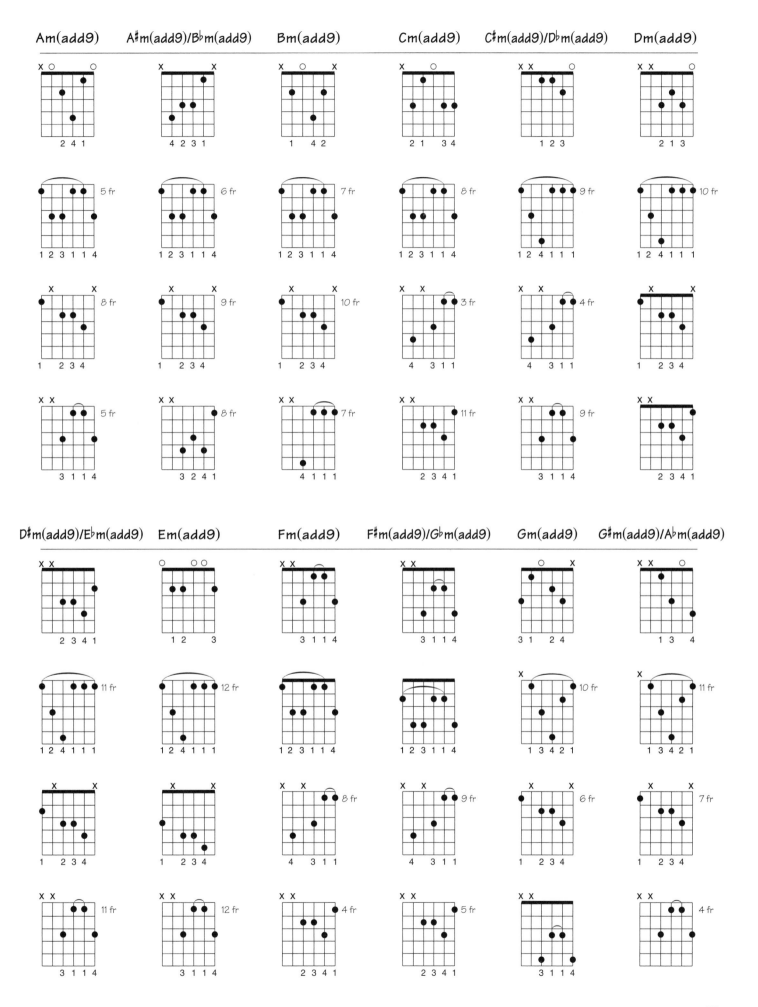

Am(add9)  A#m(add9)/B♭m(add9)  Bm(add9)  Cm(add9)  C#m(add9)/D♭m(add9)  Dm(add9)

D#m(add9)/E♭m(add9)  Em(add9)  Fm(add9)  F#m(add9)/G♭m(add9)  Gm(add9)  G#m(add9)/A♭m(add9)

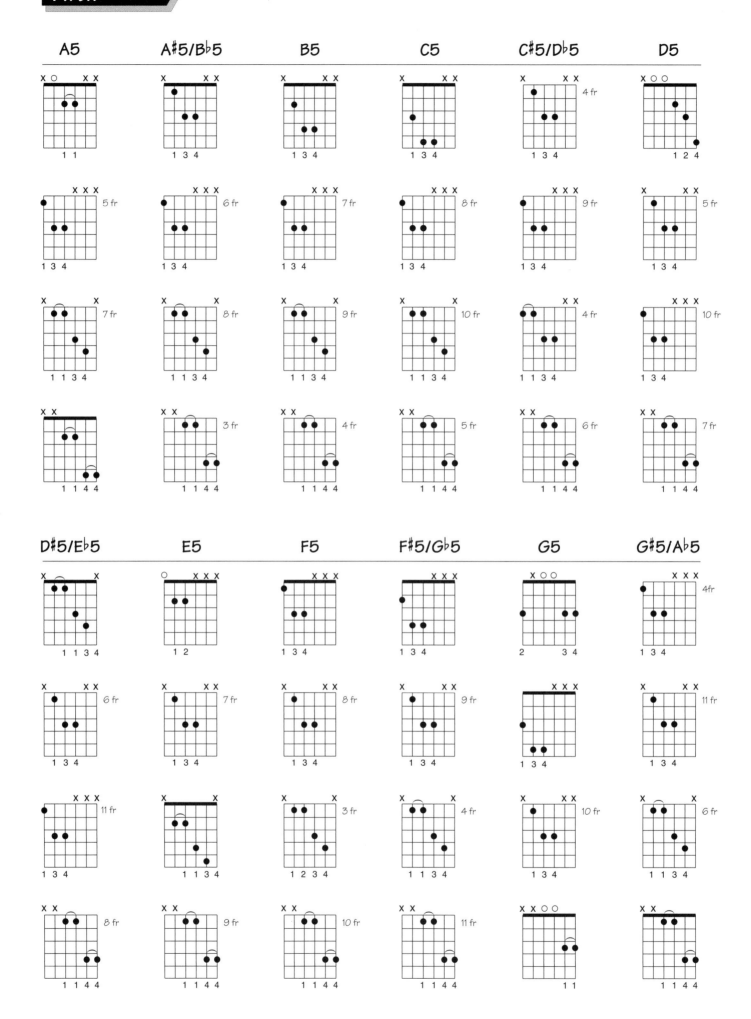

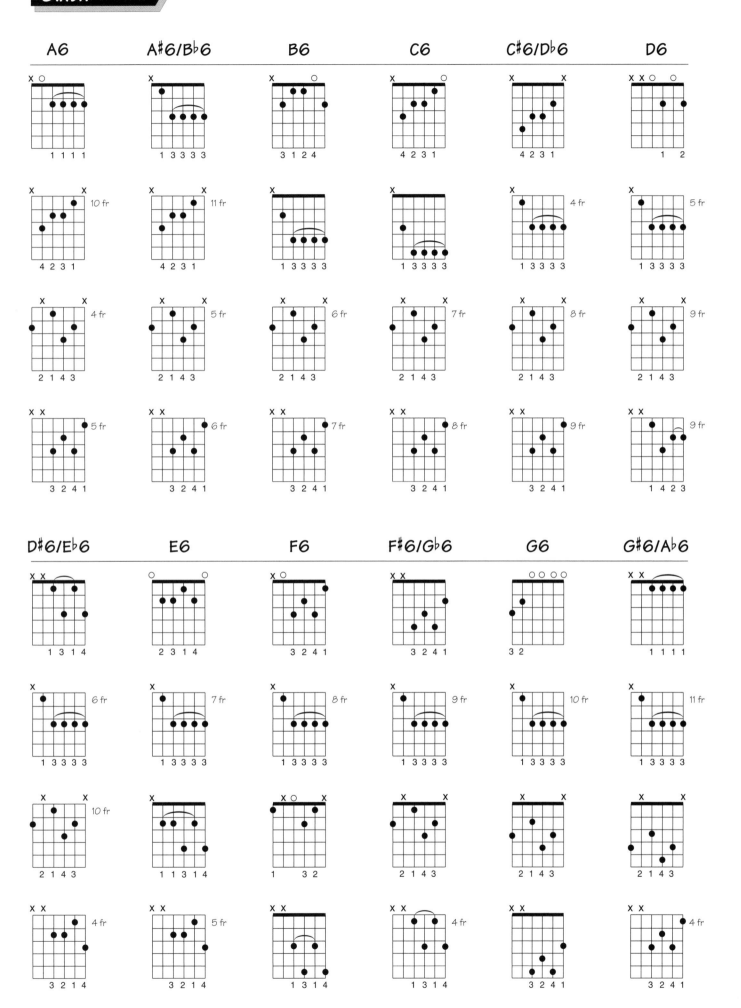

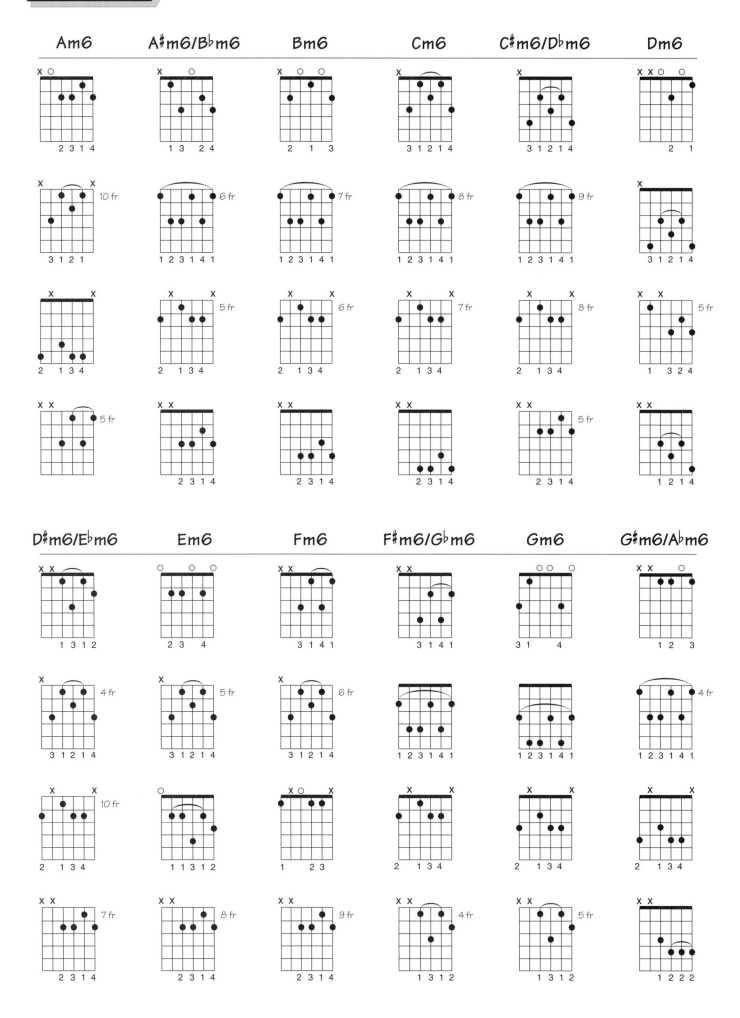

# Sixth, Added Ninth

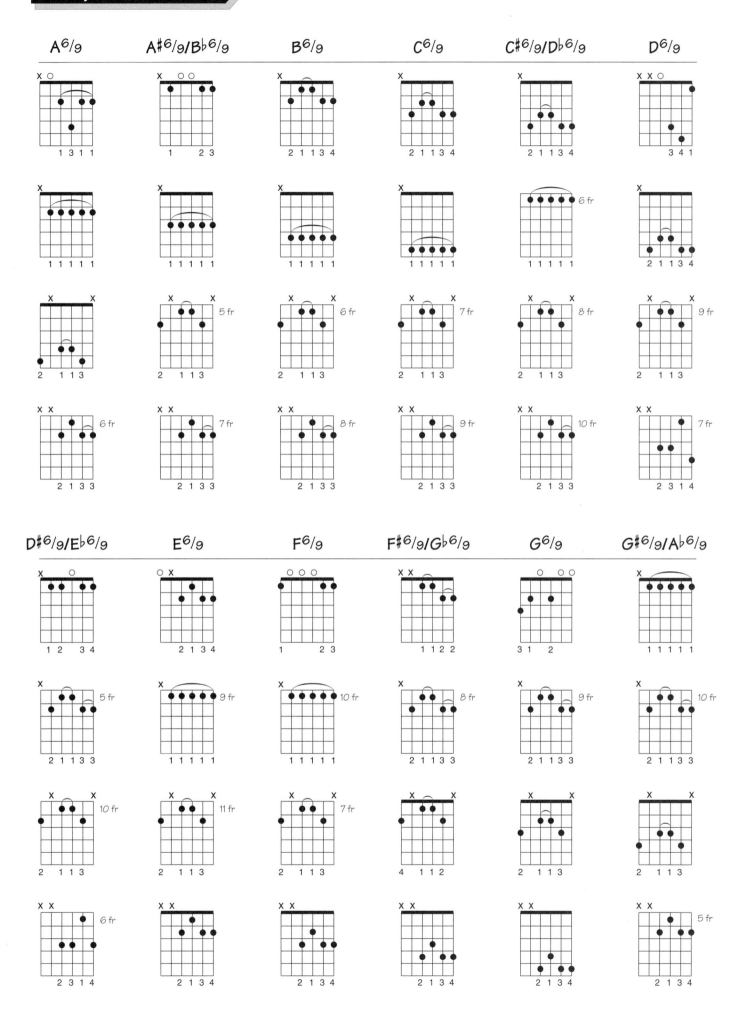

# Minor Sixth, Added Ninth

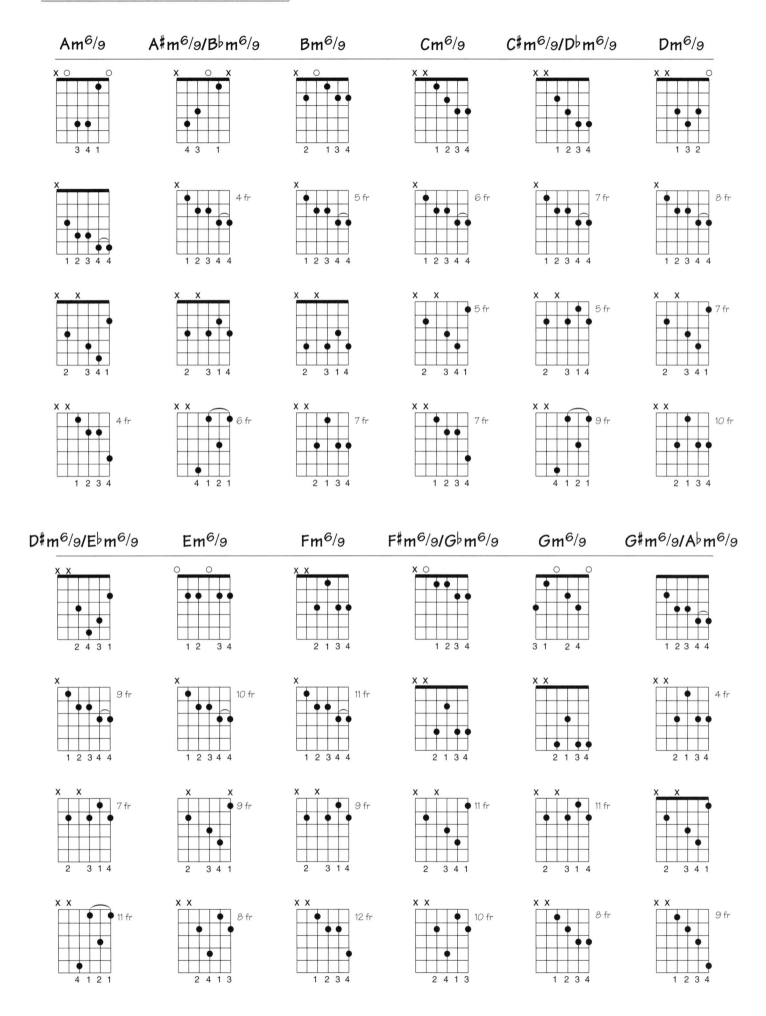

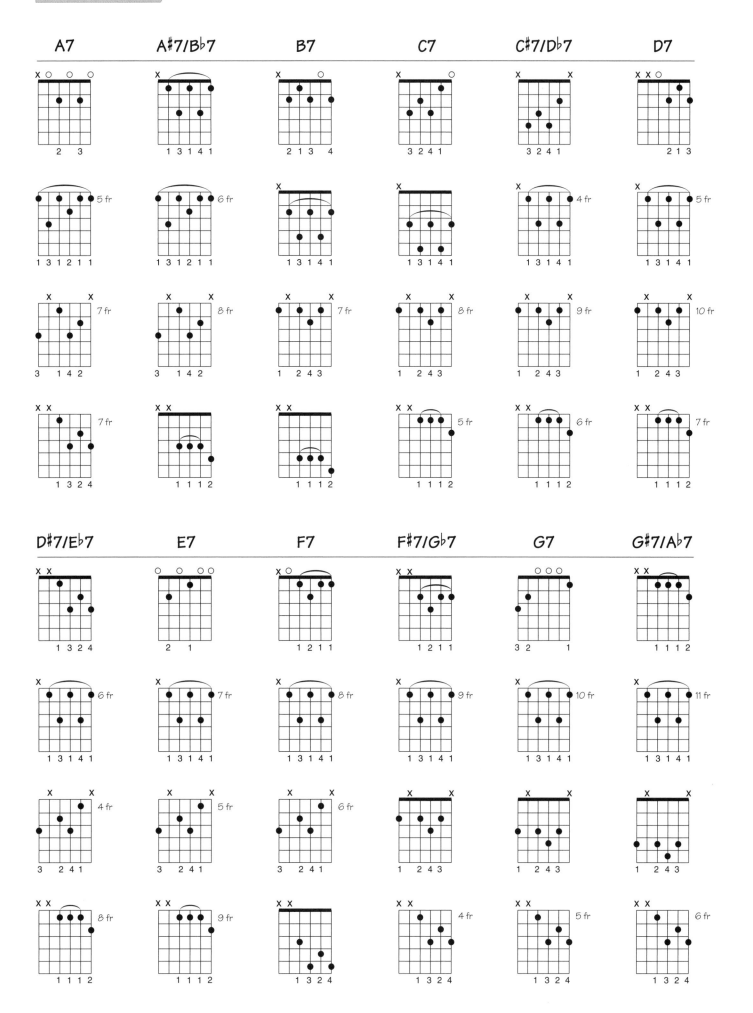

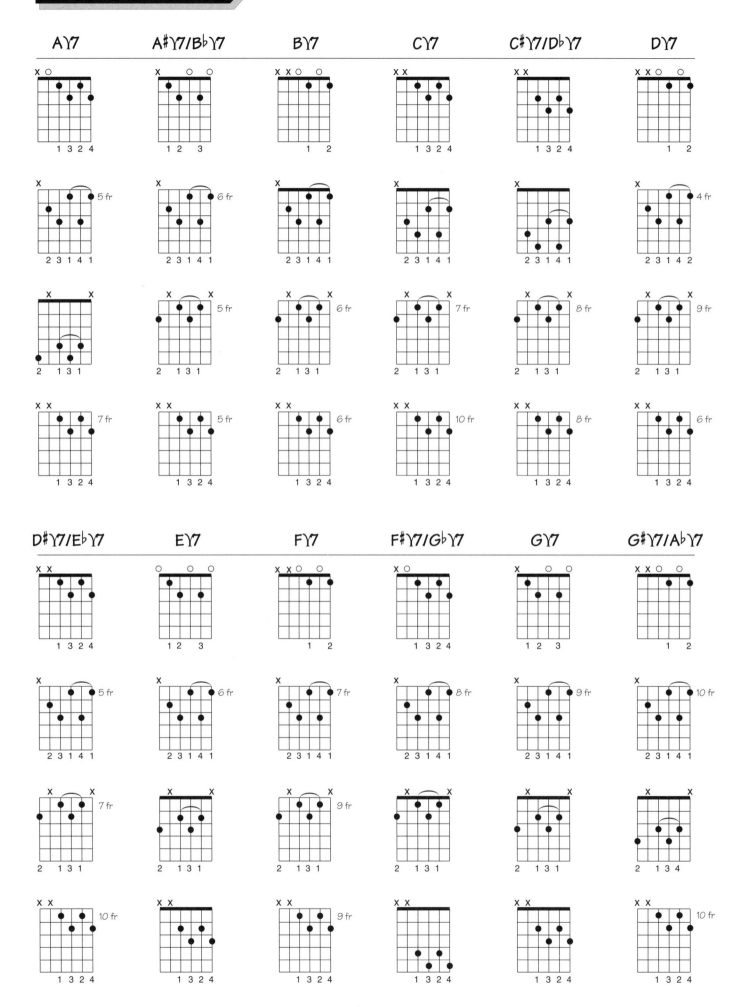

# Seventh, Suspended Fourth

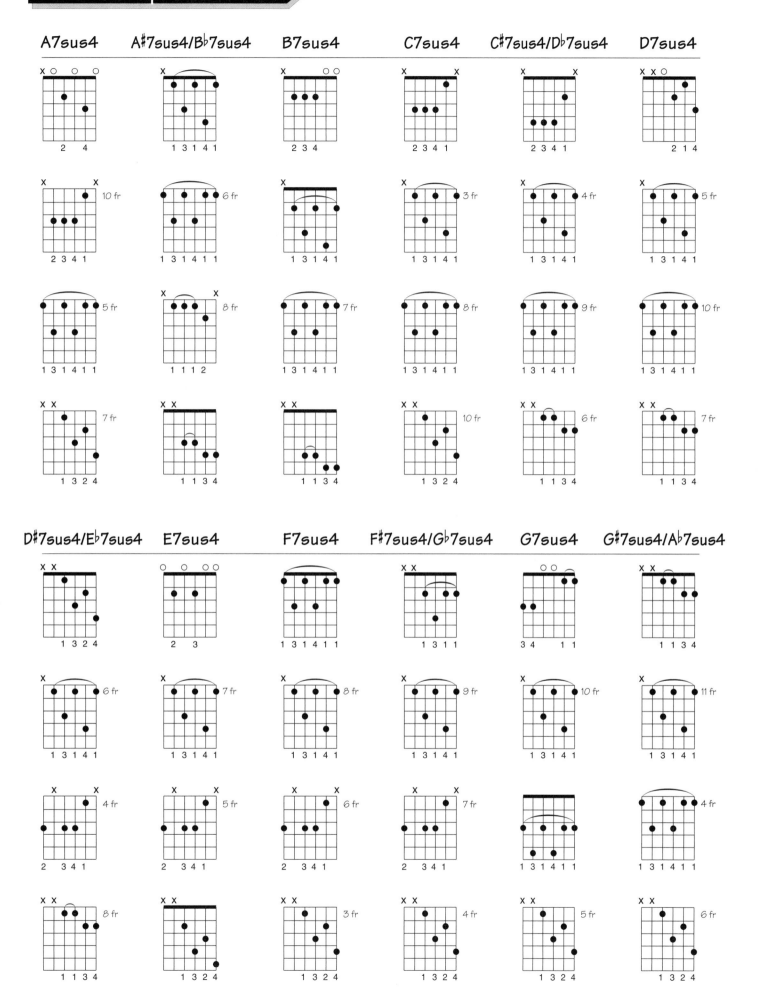

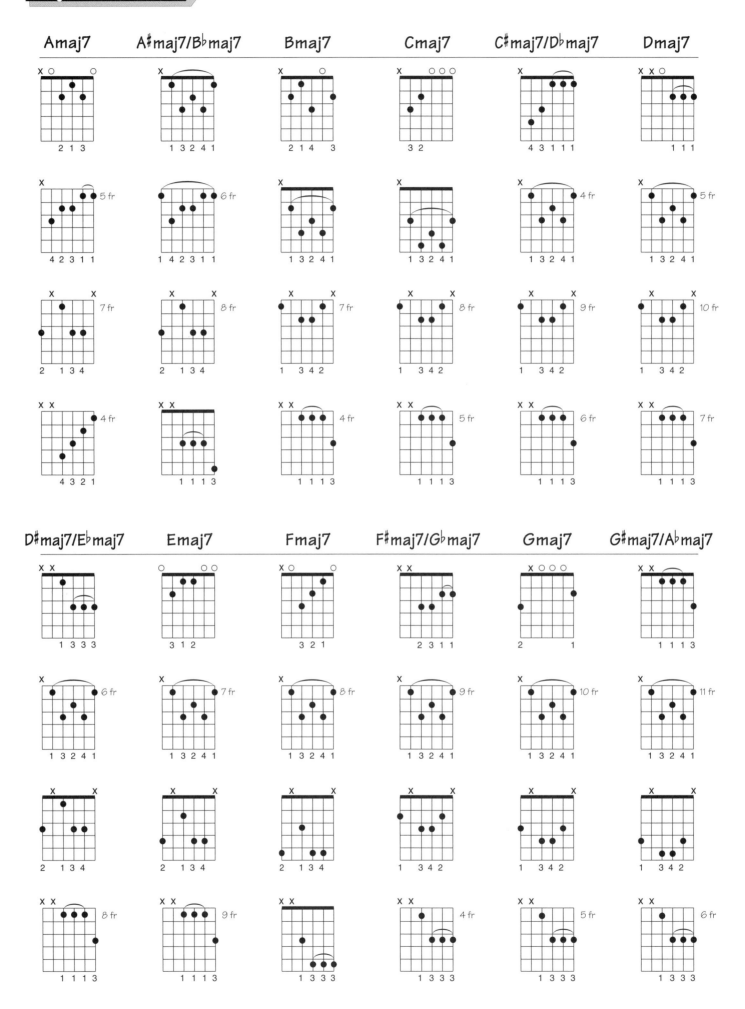

# Minor Seventh

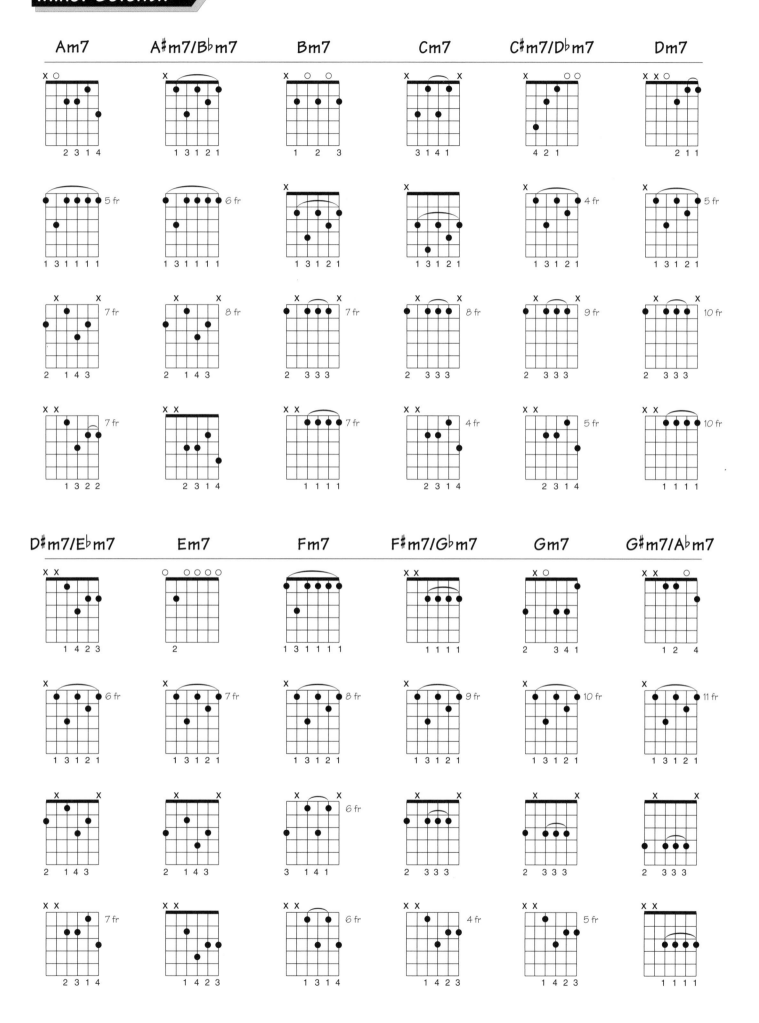

27

## Minor, Major Seventh

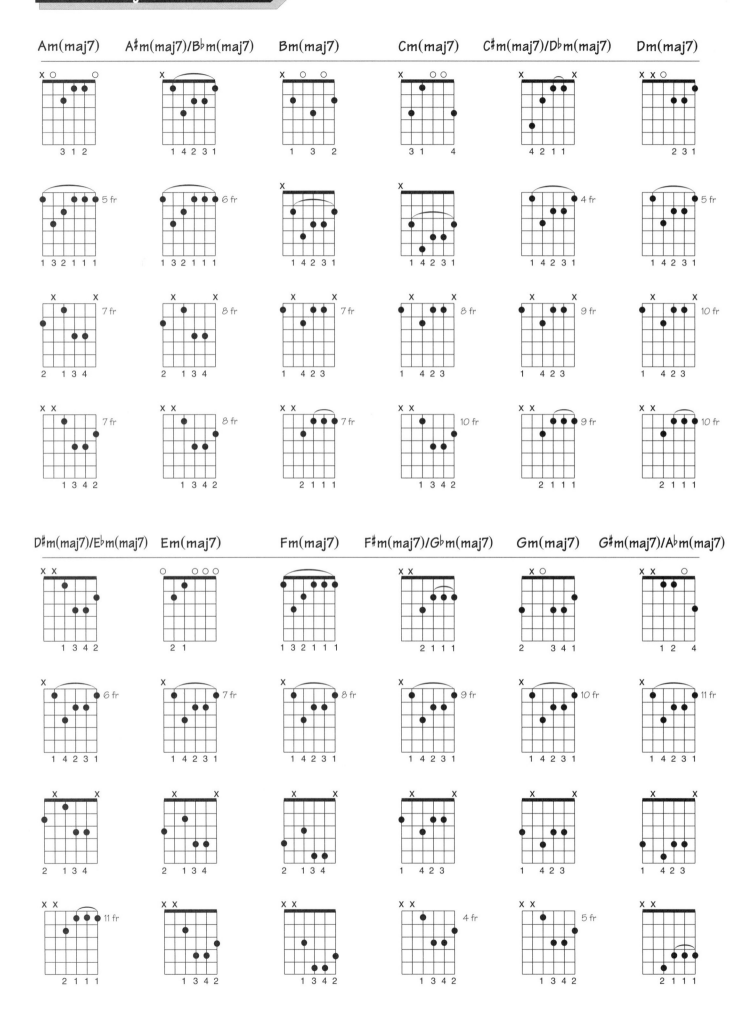

# Major Seventh, Flat Fifth

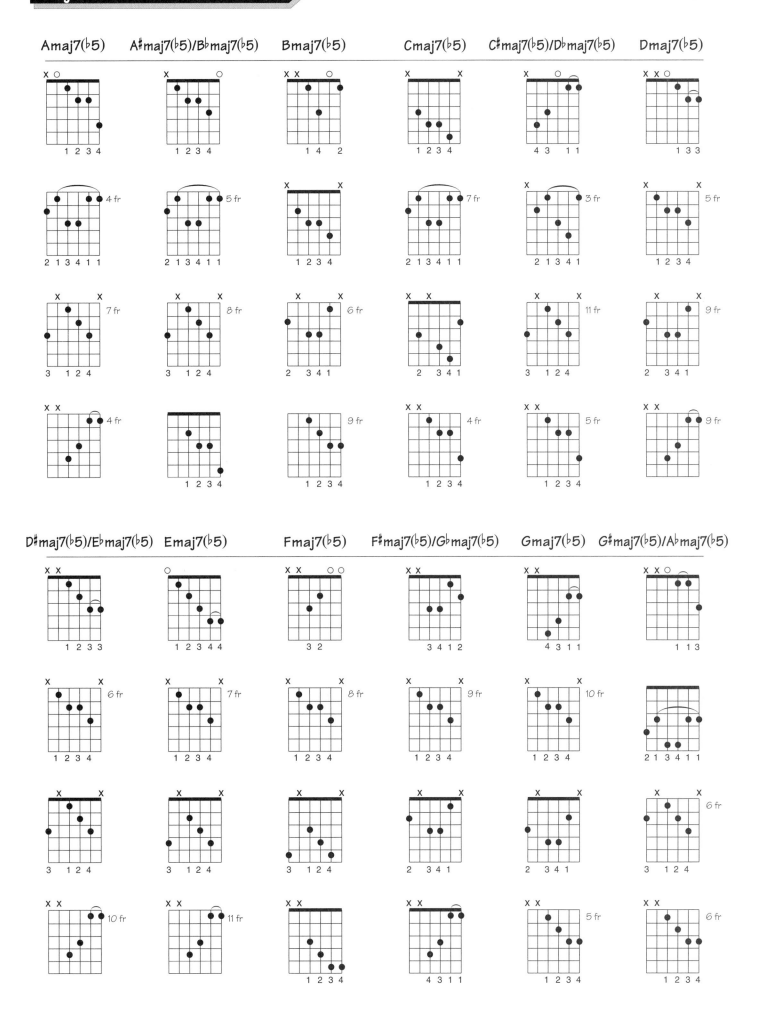

# Minor Seventh, Flat Fifth

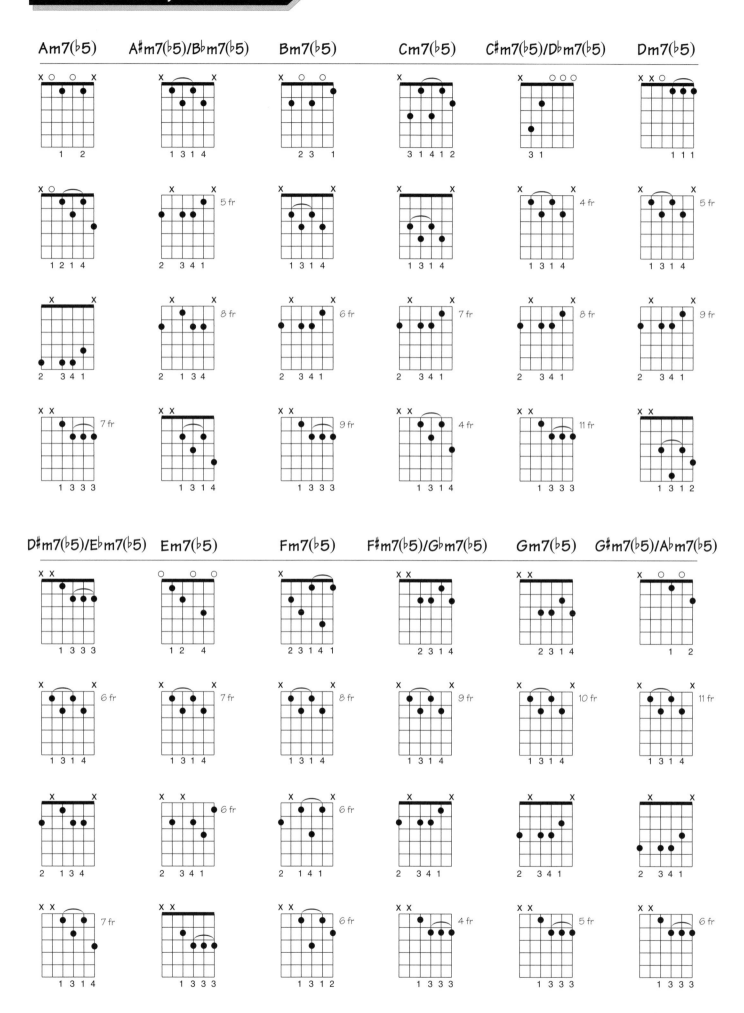

# Augmented Seventh

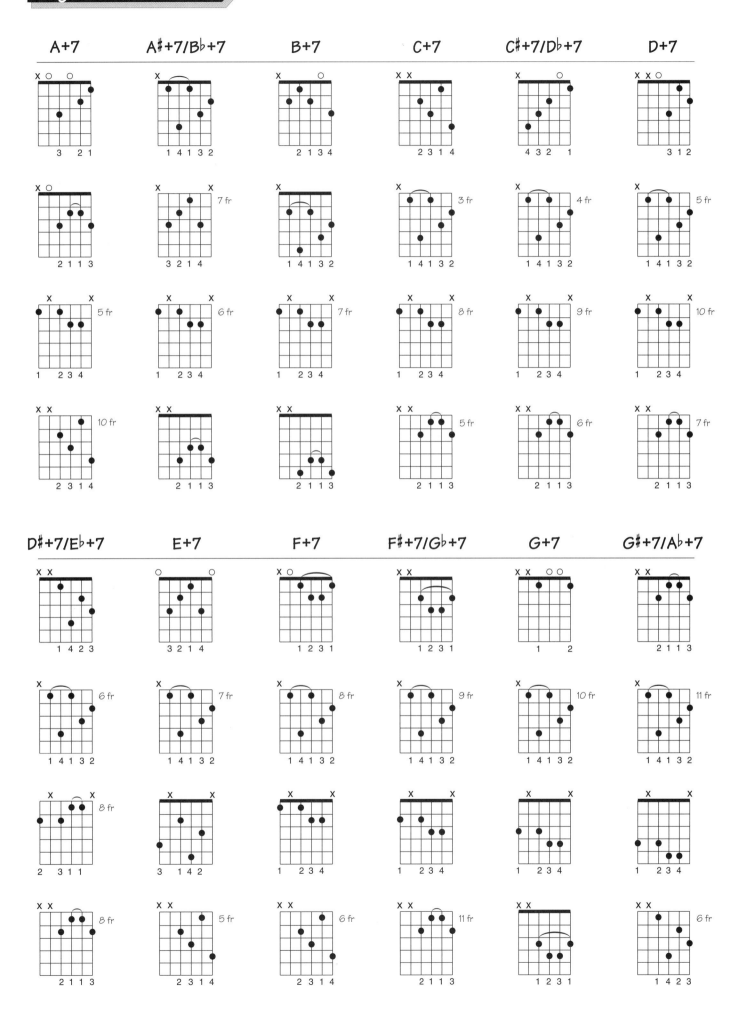

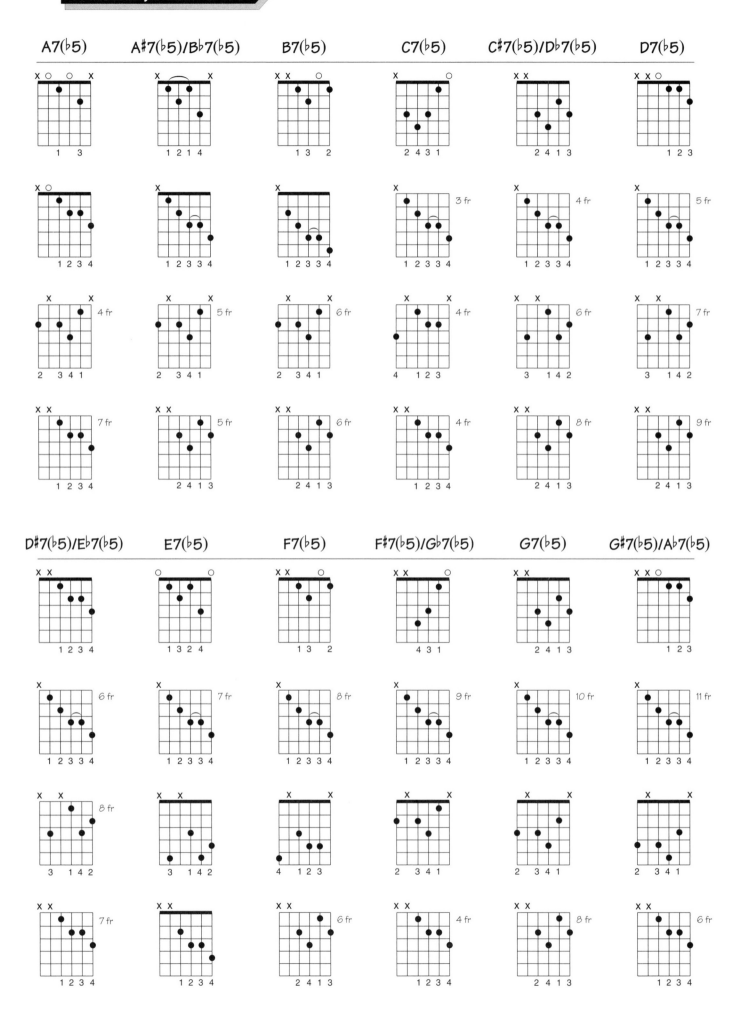

## Seventh, Flat Ninth

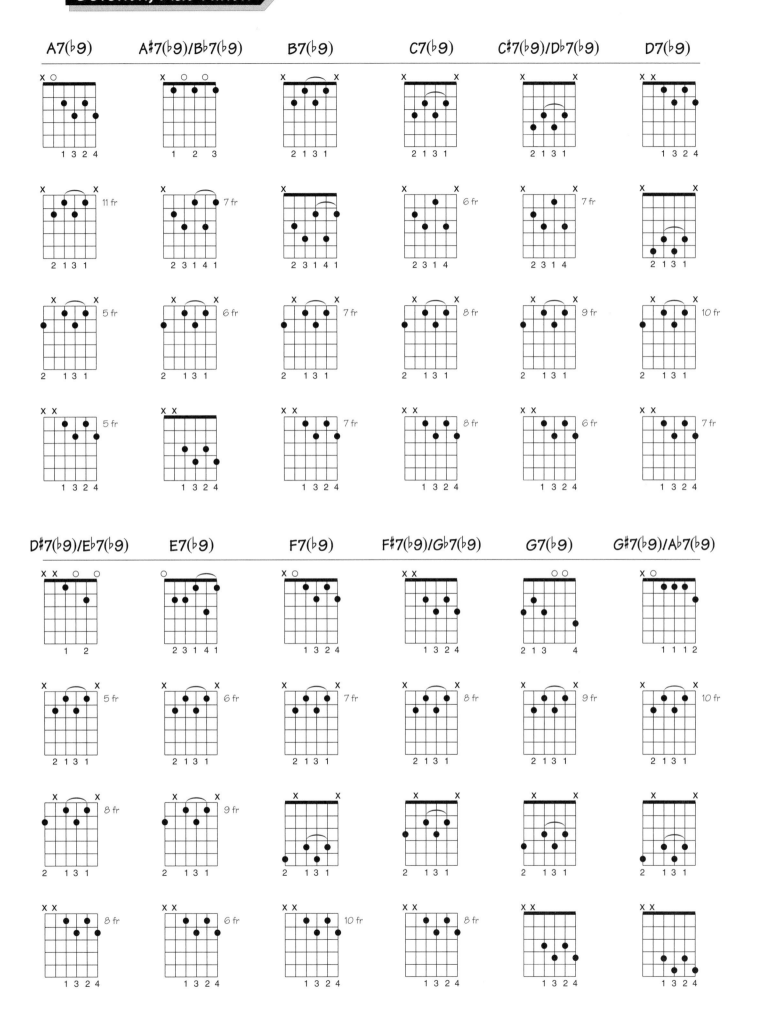

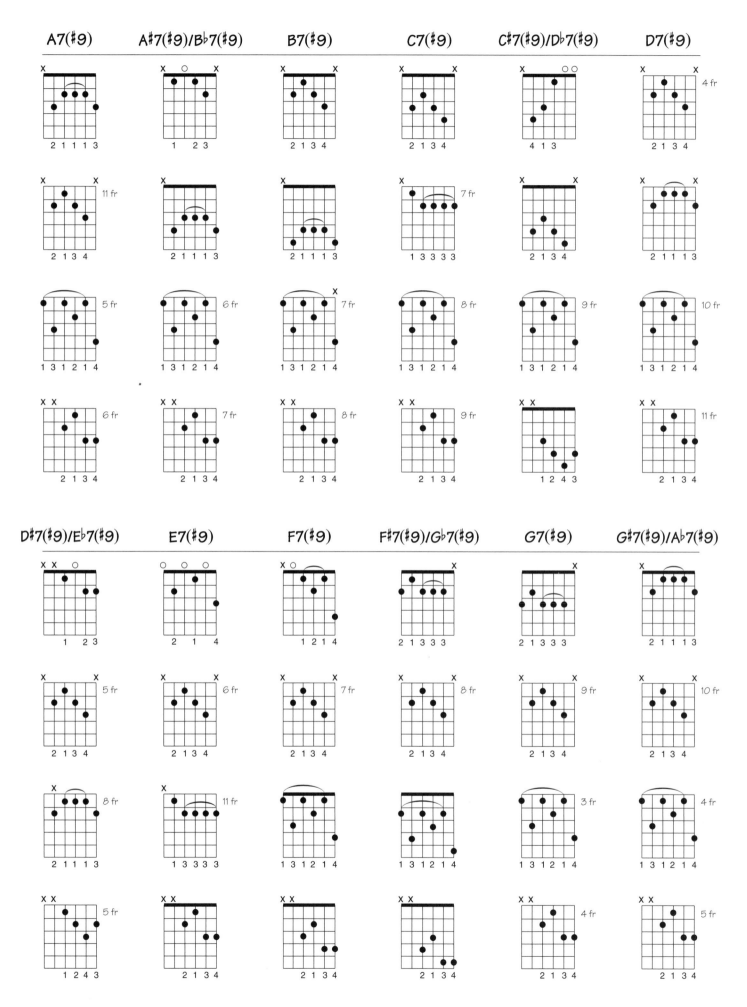

# Augmented Seventh, Flat Ninth

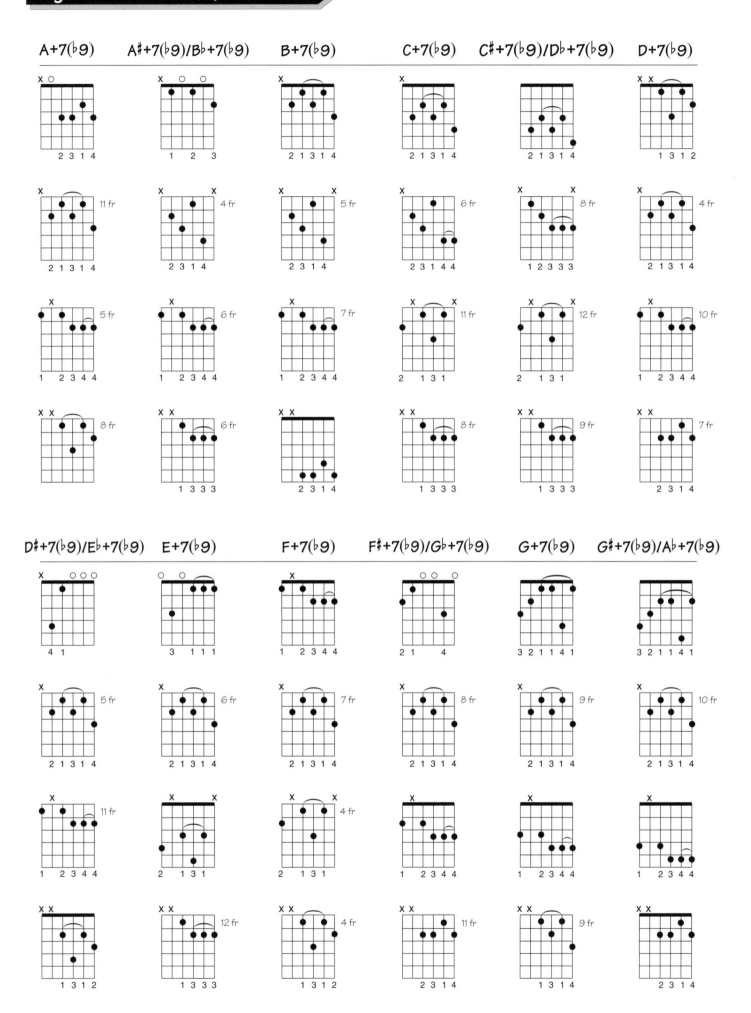

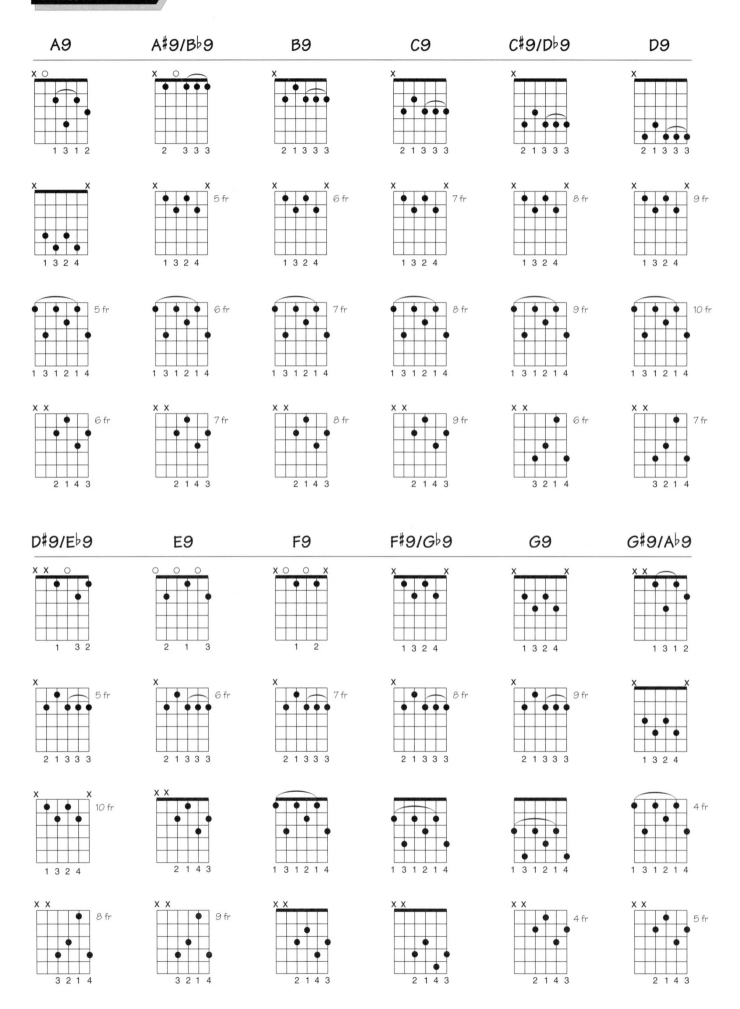

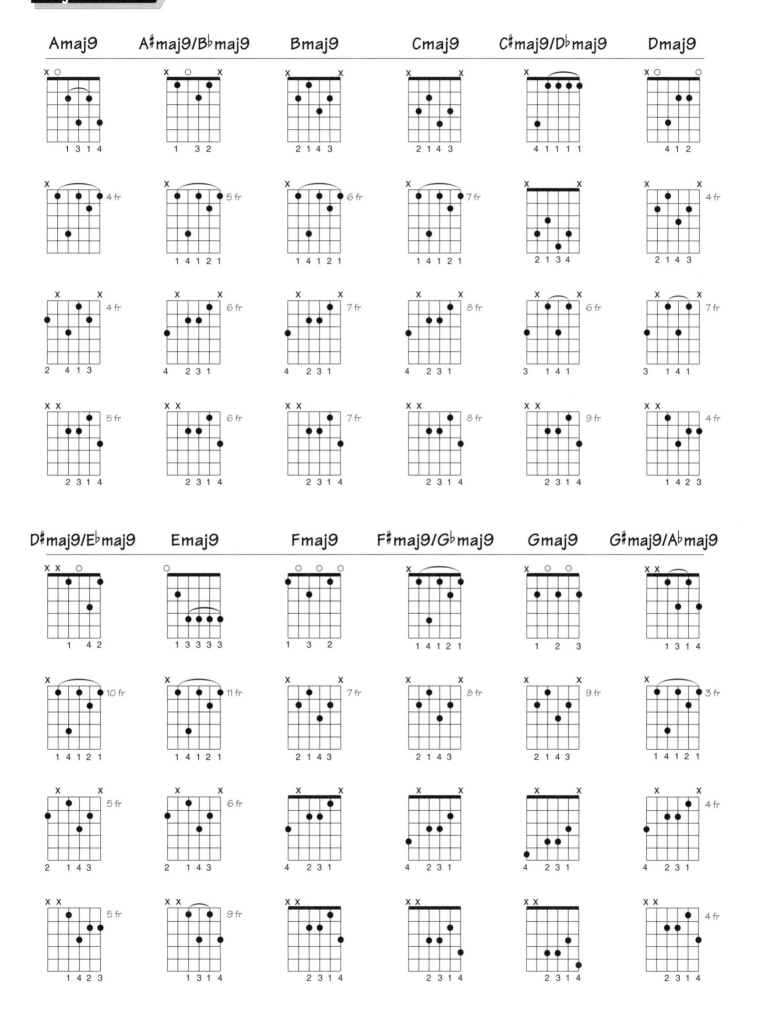

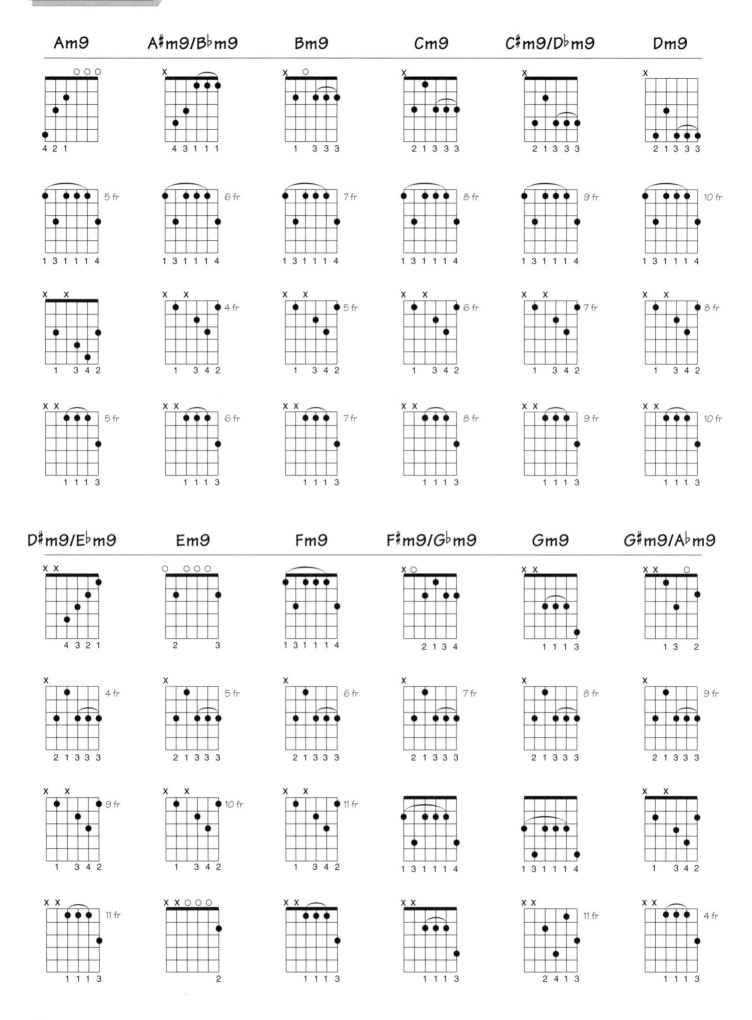

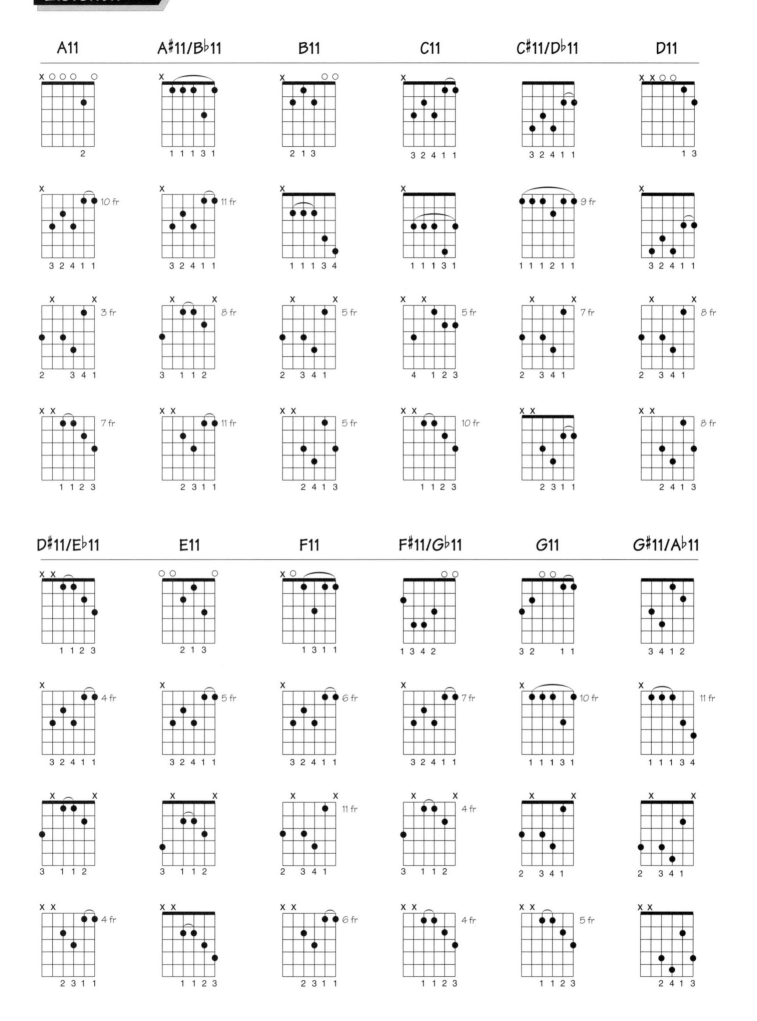

# Minor Eleventh

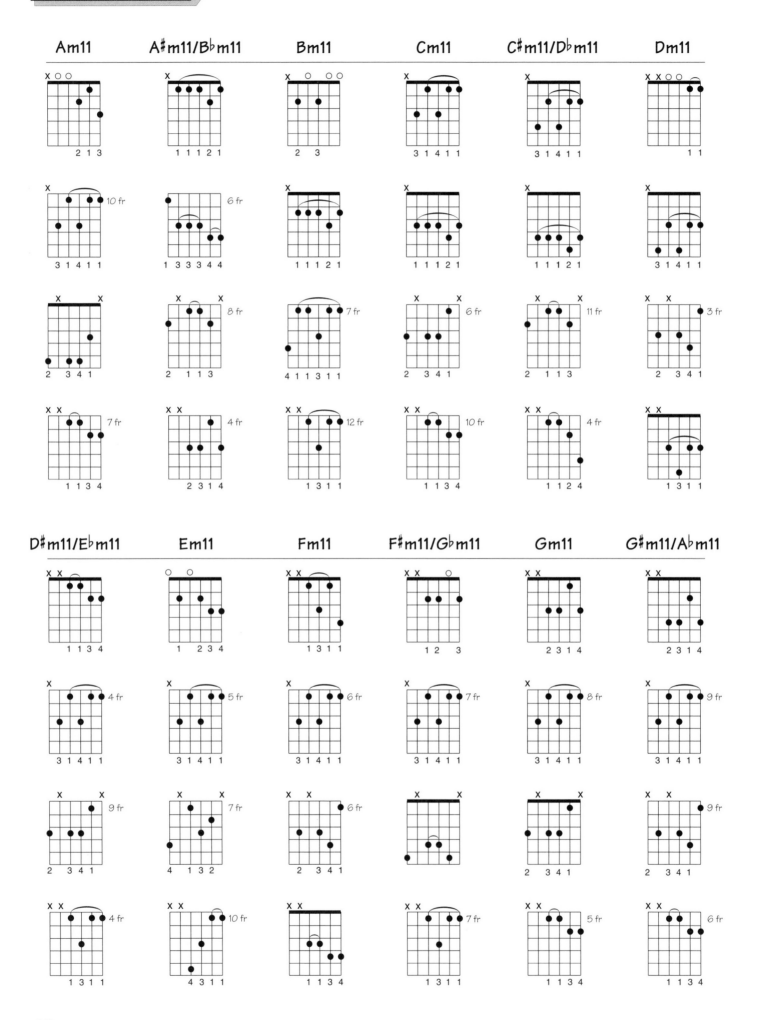

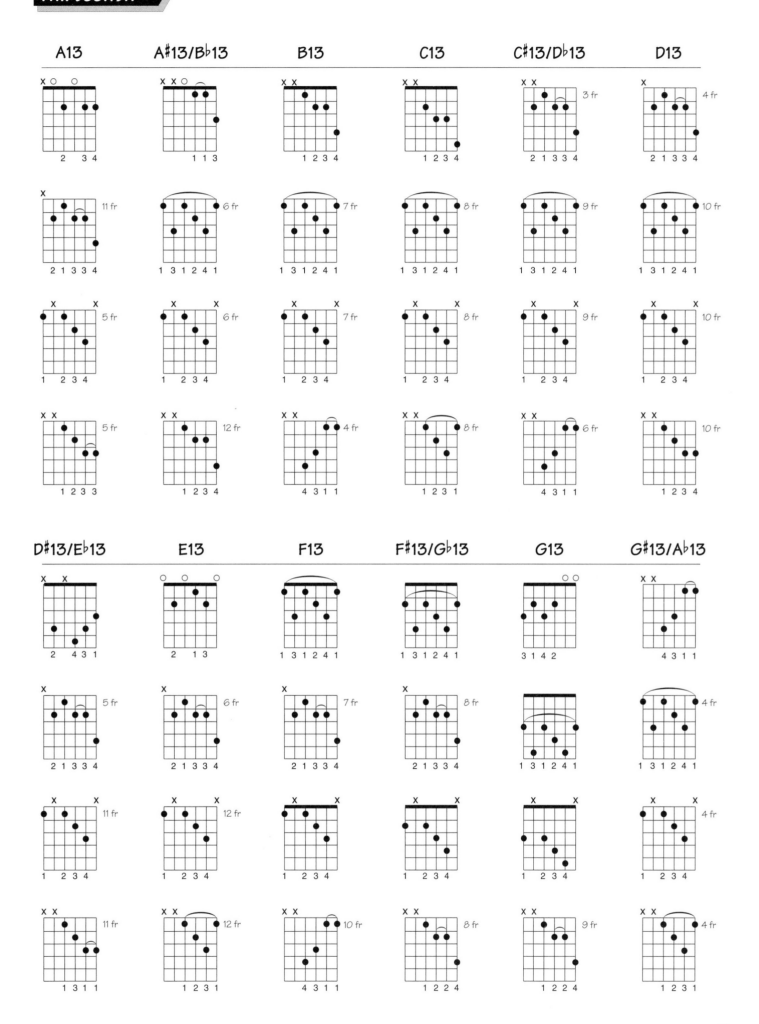

CALES

# SCALES

**Scale** (from L. *scala*, ladder): A progression of notes in a specific order.

Scales are very important to know, especially when it comes to playing a solo. This section is an easy reference for constructing, locating and playing all the essential scales on your guitar. By the end of this section, you'll be using scales to improvise over the "Jam Session" audio tracks.

## Essential ingredients...

We've given you three ways to build (or "spell") each scale:

### 1. Step Pattern    *(ex. W–H–W–W–H–W+H–H)*

This pattern tells you how many steps to move from one scale tone to the next, using abbreviations for whole step (W), half step (H) and 1 1/2 steps (W+H). Simply start on any note and move up accordingly.

Here's an example starting on the root note A:

|              |   |                      |
|--------------|---|----------------------|
| step pattern | = | W–W–H–W–W–W–H         |
| result       | = | A–B–C#–D–E–F#–G#–A    |

### 2. Formula    *(ex. 1–2–♭3–4–5–♭6–7–1)*

Take the numbers in the formula (which correspond to a particular major scale tone) and alter them as indicated by the flats and/or sharps. Try this one...

|               |   |                      |
|---------------|---|----------------------|
| A major scale | = | A–B–C#–D–E–F#–G#–A    |
| formula       | = | 1–2–♭3–4–5–♭6–7–1    |
| result        | = | A–B–C–D–E–F–G#–A      |

IMPORTANT: These formulas are always based on the **major scale** (including any sharps or flats) not just the letter names of the notes. That is, 3 for the key of E major is actually G# (not G). So, if the formula calls for ♭3, play G (one half-step lower than G#) not G♭.

### 3. Note Name    *(ex. A–B–C–D–E–F–G–A)*

Although we don't have room to show all the scales on all twelve root notes (actually seventeen if you count the enharmonics!), the note names shown are relative to the root note used. Of course, a scale built on a different root note will have a different list of note names.

# Let's get organized...

Several fretboard locations are given for each scale in this book. Use the one that feels the most comfortable for you. (Or, heck, memorize all of them!)

## Caged System

The fingerings in this system generally apply the one-finger-per-fret rule, staying within a specific four-fret position. In some cases, you may have to reach out of position one fret above or below this basic position. (Try not to hurt yourself!)

Two moveable patterns are given for each scale—one with its root on the sixth string, the other with its root on the fifth string. (For more on **moveable patterns**, flip to page 46.)

## Three-Notes-Per-String System

These require a bit more of a stretch but generally span a full 2 1/2 octaves. Two moveable fingerings are given for each scale. Again, one with a sixth string root and one with a fifth string root.

## Horizontal System

Depending on the scale, these are found as either sliding scales, or four-notes-per-string patterns. The fingerings in this system spread up to 16 frets (Ouch!), but they're handy in trying to connect distant areas of the fretboard or to smoothly transfer from one position to another.

Like the **caged** and **three-notes-per-string** systems, two moveable patterns also accompany each scale in the **horizontal** system.

# Get in sync!

Practicing scales requires both hands to work together in perfect synchronization. Strike each note clearly and precisely, making sure you pick and finger the note at exactly the same time. Remember to always use **alternate picking** (successive downstroke and upstroke attacks) to avoid excessive hand strain.

☞ **PRACTICE TIP:** Make sure you play each scale forward and then backward. And, as always, start out slow and gradually build up speed as you build up confidence.

# MOVEABLE PATTERNS

**A**ll of the scale patterns given in this book are **moveable**—that is, they can be easily shifted up or down the fingerboard to accomodate any key or root note. To do this, take note of the darkened root notes:

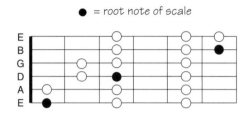

You can use any of these root notes as a point of reference for moving patterns. However, the roots located on the fifth and sixth strings are usually the easiest places to start.

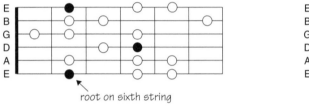

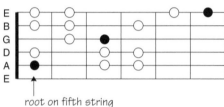

To play the scale pattern in any particular key, match one of the root notes to its respective note on the fingerboard. (For example, the key of C has a root note of C.) The rest of the pattern follows accordingly—it's as simple as shifting the shape.

Check out the example below:

| Moveable Major Scale Pattern | Beginning Fret (fret the root is on) | Resulting Scale |
|:---:|:---:|:---:|
| | fret 1 | F major scale |
| | fret 3 | G major scale |
| | fret 6 | Bb major scale |
| | fret 10 | D major scale |
| | fret 12 | E major scale |

# Picture this...

Use the **Guitar Fingerboard Chart** below to help you quickly locate all the notes within the first twelve frets. As described on the previous page, this chart will be especially useful as you begin using the moveable scale patterns in the pages ahead.

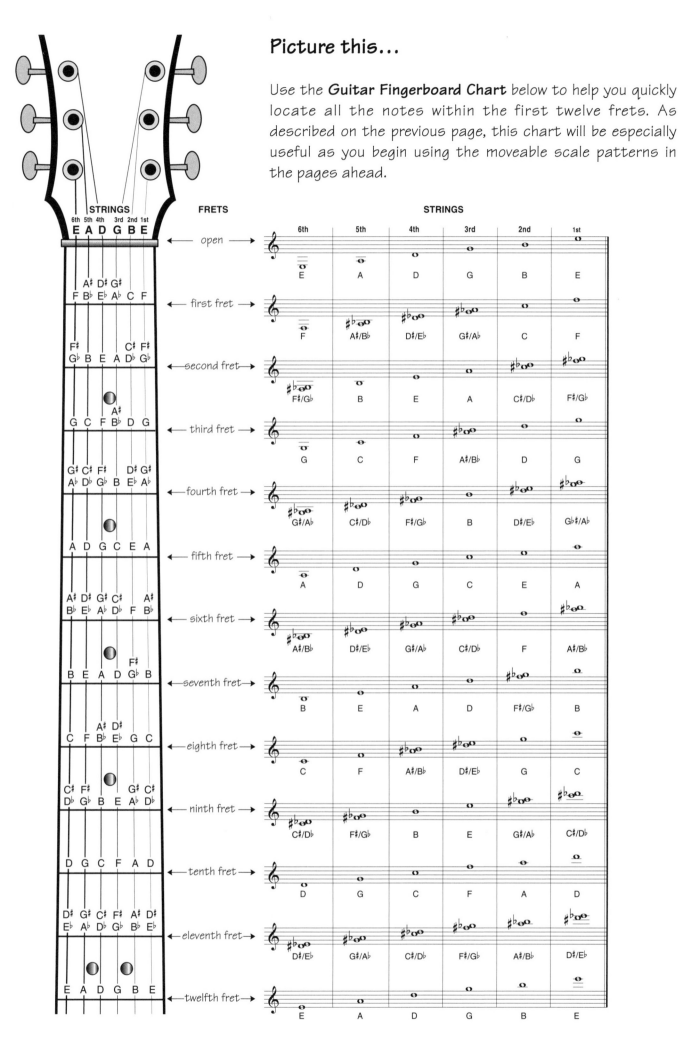

# MAJOR

The most common scale used in music is the major scale, so learn it well! It consists of eight consecutive notes ascending or descending.

Step pattern:  W–W–H–W–W–W–H

Formula:  1–2–3–4–5–6–7–1

Notes:  C–D–E–F–G–A–B–C

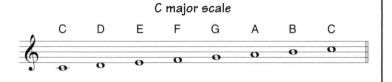

IMPORTANT: Scale patterns played on the guitar cover all of the notes within a certain fretboard area. In other words, the notes in the scale are repeated in different octaves for a more complete and practical fingering.

## Caged System

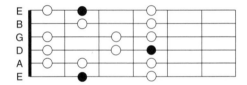
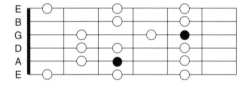

## Three-Notes-Per-String System

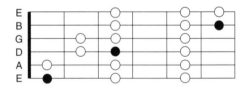
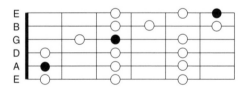

## Horizontal System

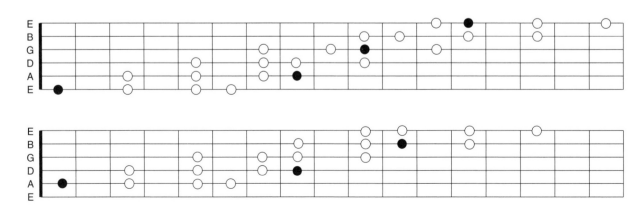

48

# MINOR

This scale is used in nearly all styles of Western music. It's sometimes referred to as the "pure minor," "relative minor," or "Aeolian mode."

Step pattern: W–H–W–W–H–W–W

Formula: 1–2–♭3–4–5–♭6–♭7–1

Notes: C–D–E♭–F–G–A♭–B♭–C

C natural minor scale

## Caged System

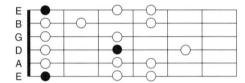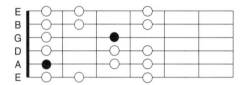

## Three-Notes-Per-String System

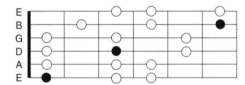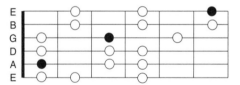

## Horizontal System

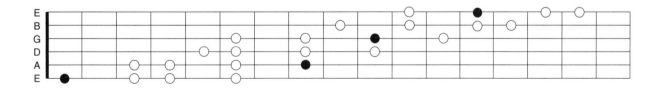

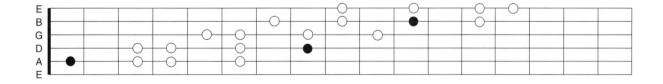

# HARMONIC MINOR

This scale provides another alternative minor scale type and is very common in classical music.

Step pattern: W–H–W–W–H–W+H–H

Formula: 1–2–♭3–4–5–♭6–7–8

Notes: C–D–E♭–F–G–A♭–B–C

C harmonic minor scale

C   D   E♭   F   G   A♭   B   C

## Caged System

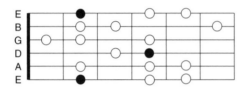

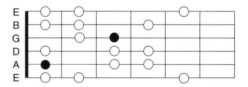

## Three-Notes-Per-String System

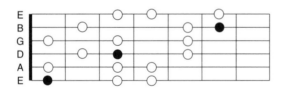

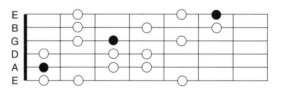

## Horizontal System

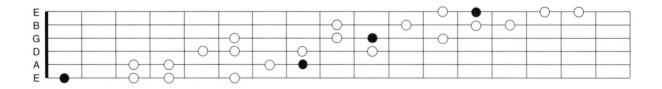

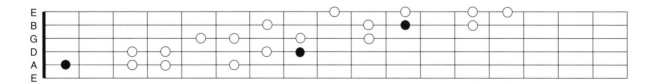

# MELODIC MINOR

This scale can also be used over minor chords and is commonly referred to as the "jazz minor" scale.

Step pattern: W–H–W–W–W–W–H

Formula: 1–2–♭3–4–5–6–7–8

Notes: C–D–E♭–F–G–A–B–C

C melodic minor scale

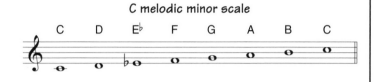

## Caged System

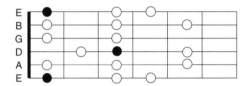
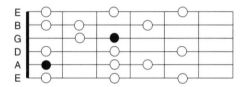

## Three-Notes-Per-String System

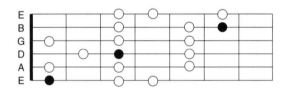
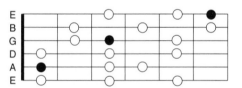

## Horizontal System

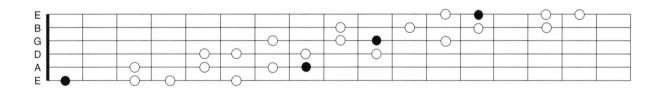

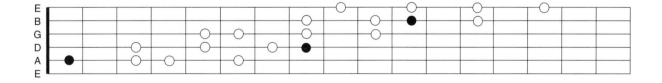

# MINOR PENTATONIC

This is undeniably the most prevalent scale used by rock and blues players. As its name suggests ("penta" means five), this scale contains only five different tones.

Step pattern: W+H–W–W–W+H–W

Formula: 1–♭3–4–5–♭7

Notes: C–E♭–F–G–B♭–C

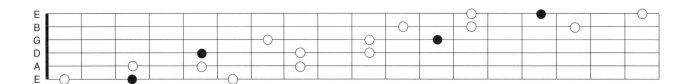
C minor pentatonic scale

## Caged System

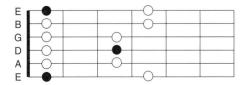
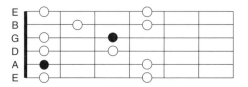

## Three-Notes-Per-String System

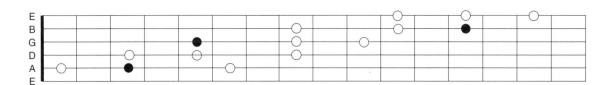

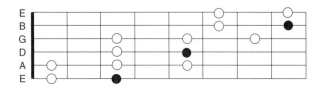

## Horizontal System

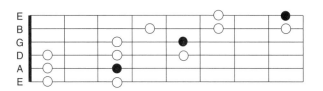

# MAJOR PENTATONIC

This is another 5-tone ("pentatonic") scale common in many styles of music. It has a "bright" sound that especially lends itself well to country music.

Step pattern: W–W–W+H–W–W+H

Formula: 1–2–3–5–6–1

Notes: C–D–E–G–A–C

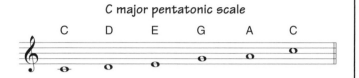

C major pentatonic scale

C   D   E   G   A   C

## Caged System

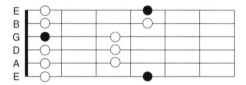

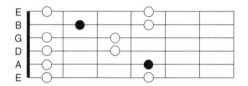

## Three-Notes-Per-String System

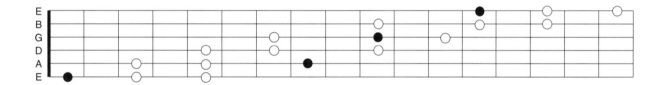

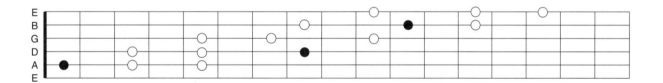

## Horizontal System

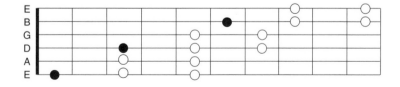

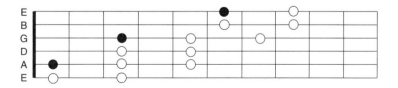

# BLUES

The blues scale is common in jazz, rock, and (you guessed it!) **blues music**. It's a six-note scale that's just like the minor pentatonic but with an added ♭5 "blues note."

Step pattern: W+H–W–H–H–W+H–W

Formula: 1–♭3–4–♭5–5–♭7–1

Notes: C–E♭–F–G♭–G–B♭–C

C blues scale

## Caged System

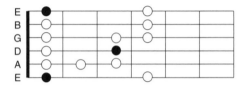 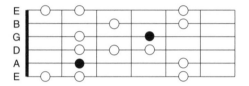

## Three-Notes-Per-String System

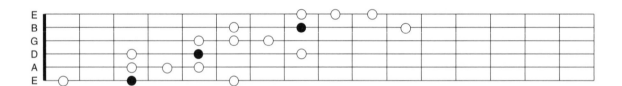

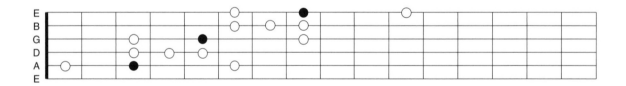

## Horizontal System

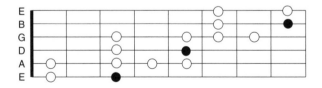

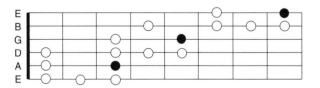

54

# DIMINISHED

This scale is popular in jazz and heavy metal music (turn it up!). NOTE: It's not a typo, there really are eight different tones in this scale.

Step pattern: W–H–W–H–W–H–W–H

Formula: 1–2–♭3–4–♭5–♭6–6–7–8

Notes: C–D–E♭–F–G♭–A♭–A–B–C

C diminished scale

## Caged System

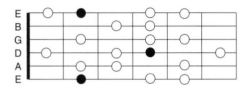
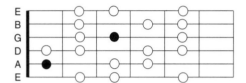

## Three-Notes-Per-String System

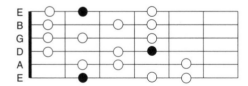
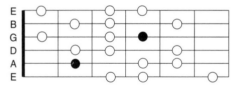

## Horizontal System

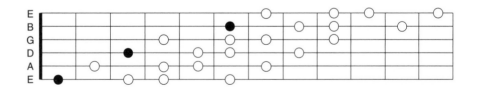

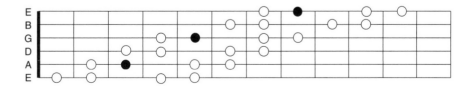

# MODES

Modes are like scales—each uses a specific pattern of whole steps and half steps. The difference is that a mode is not related to the key of its root note. That is, a Dorian mode built on C is not in the key of C. The seven modes in common practice today are derived from the seven notes of the major scale:

```
                             W   W   H   W   W   W   H
                             ∧   ∧   ∧   ∧   ∧   ∧   ∧
C Ionian        =   C   D   E   F   G   A   B   C
(same as C major)


                         W   H   W   W   W   H   W
                         ∧   ∧   ∧   ∧   ∧   ∧   ∧
D Dorian        =   D   E   F   G   A   B   C   D


                       H   W   W   W   H   W   W
                       ∧   ∧   ∧   ∧   ∧   ∧   ∧
E Phrygian     =   E   F   G   A   B   C   D   E


                           W   W   W   H   W   W   H
                           ∧   ∧   ∧   ∧   ∧   ∧   ∧
F Lydian        =   F   G   A   B   C   D   E   F


                             W   W   H   W   W   H   W
                             ∧   ∧   ∧   ∧   ∧   ∧   ∧
G Mixolydian =   G   A   B   C   D   E   F   G


                           W   H   W   W   H   W   W
                           ∧   ∧   ∧   ∧   ∧   ∧   ∧
A Aeolian       =   A   B   C   D   E   F   G   A
(same as A natural minor)


                         H   W   W   H   W   W   W
                         ∧   ∧   ∧   ∧   ∧   ∧   ∧
B Locrian      =   B   C   D   E   F   G   A   B
```

As you can see, each mode is actually a variation of the major scale. They differ only in the arrangement of the intervals.

The next page gives you two usable patterns for each of the seven modes...

## Ionian

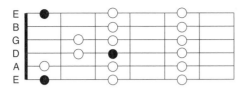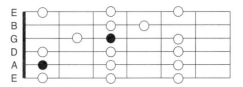

## Dorian

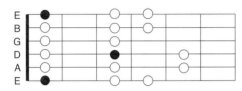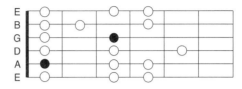

## Phrygian

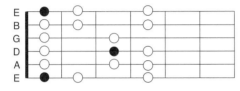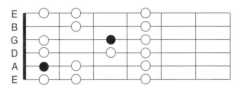

## Lydian

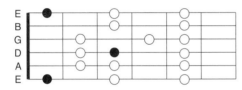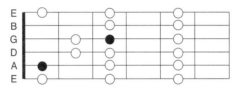

## Mixolydian

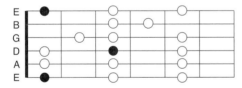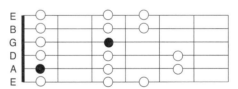

## Aeolian

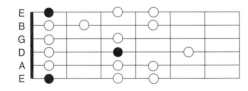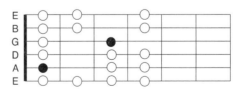

## Locrian

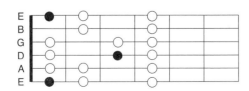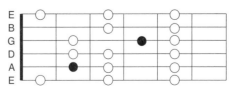

# JAM SESSION

# JAM SESSION
## *Time to charge admission...*

Now it's time to use the chords and scales from this book and make some **actual music!** This section provides twenty chord progressions found in various music styles. Play along with the audio. You can either follow the chord symbols and strum along, or use the suggested scales to practice improvising.

### Heavenly Ballad

suggested scales: G major, G major pentatonic, E minor pentatonic

| G | D | C | D | *play 8 times* | G |

### Medium Rock

suggested scales: E minor, E minor pentatonic

| Em | D | C | | *play 8 times* | Em |

### Wall of Fame

suggested scales: D minor, D minor pentatonic, D blues

| Dm | A5  C5  Dm | *play 8 times* |

### Wild and Crazy

suggested scales: A minor pentatonic, A blues

| A5  D5 | E5  D5 | *play 8 times* | A5 |

## Full Deck Shuffle

suggested scales: E blues, E minor pentatonic

E                                                                                    A

‖: / / / / | / / / / | / / / / | / / / / | / / / / | / / / / |

E                          B              A              E              B   play 3 times   E

| / / / / | / / / / | / / / / | / / / / | / / / / | / / / / :‖ ◇ ‖

## Generic Pop

suggested scales: C major, C major pentatonic

C       Am        F       G      play 8 times   C

‖: / / / / | / / / / :‖ ◇ ‖

## Funky Feeling

suggested scales: E blues, E minor pentatonic

E9                        A9     play 8 times   E9

‖: / / / / | / / / / :‖ ◇ ‖

## Don't Stop

suggested scales: G major, G major pentatonic

G     C        Am       D  play 8 times   G

‖: / / / / | / / / / :‖ ◇ ‖

## Smooth Jazz

suggested scales: F major, F major pentatonic

Fmaj7             B♭maj7               Gm7                C7        play 8 times   Fmaj7

‖: / / / / | / / / / | / / / / | / / / / :‖ ◇ ‖

## Overtime

suggested scales: C blues, C minor pentatonic

C                  B♭                 F                  C      play 8 times   C

‖: / / / / | / / / / | / / / / | / / / / :‖ ◇ ‖

### Nashville Dreamin'

suggested scales: C major pentatonic, C major

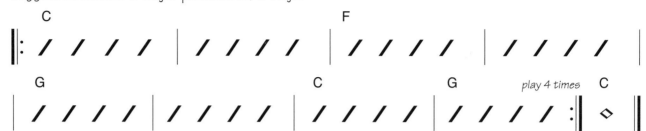

### Heavy Rock

suggested scales: E Dorian, E minor penatonic

### Alley Cat

suggested scales: (first three measures): A minor, A minor pentatonic
suggested scales: (fourth measure): A harmonic minor

### Fusion

suggested scales: C Phrygian, C minor pentatonic

### South of the Border

suggested scales: G blues, G minor, G minor pentatonic, G harmonic minor

## Scare Us

suggested scales: B♭ Lydian, A minor pentatonic

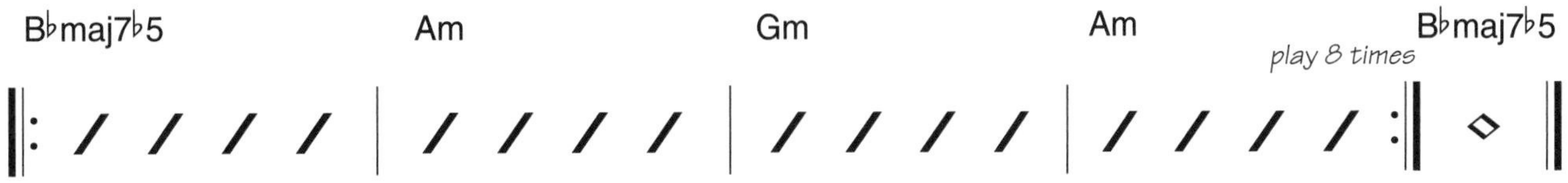

B♭maj7♭5      Am      Gm      Am      B♭maj7♭5

*play 8 times*

‖: / / / / | / / / / | / / / / | / / / / :‖ ◇ ‖

## Swing It!

suggested scales: C Ionian, C major

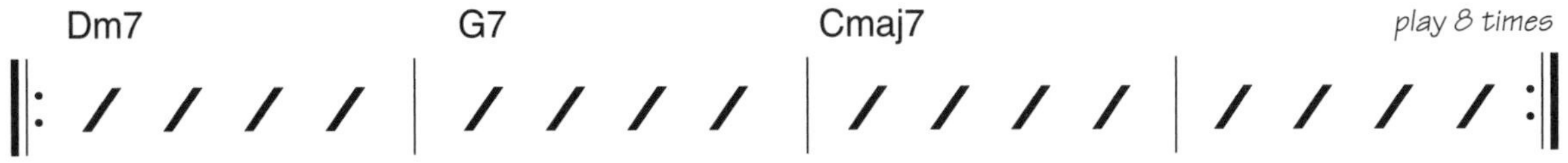

Dm7      G7      Cmaj7

*play 8 times*

‖: / / / / | / / / / | / / / / | / / / / :‖

## Metal Mix

suggested scales: F♯ Aeolian, F♯ minor pentatonic

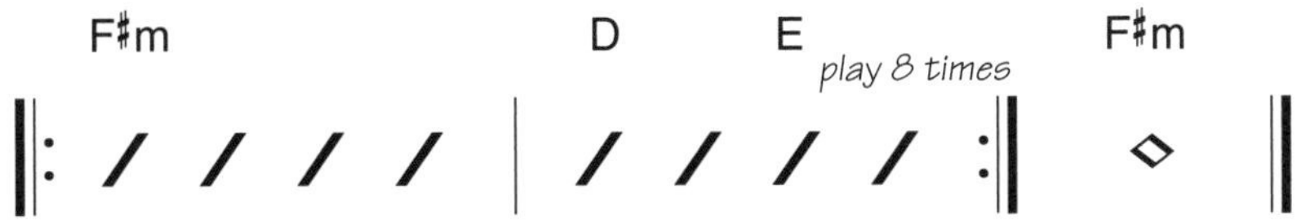

F♯m      D    E      F♯m

*play 8 times*

‖: / / / / | / / / / :‖ ◇ ‖

## Rock 'n' Roll

suggested scales: D major, D major pentatonic

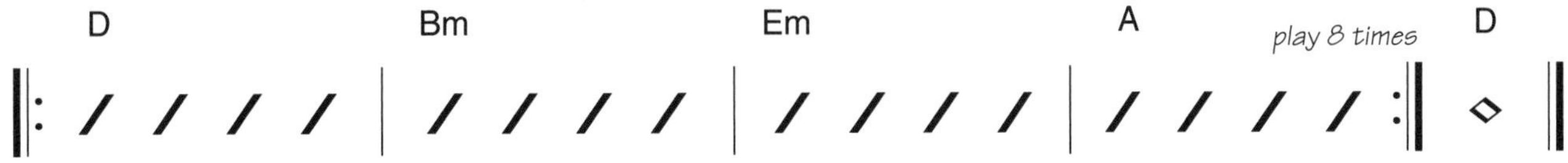

D      Bm      Em      A      D

*play 8 times*

‖: / / / / | / / / / | / / / / | / / / / :‖ ◇ ‖

## Outta Here

suggested scales: E Mixolydian, E major pentatonic

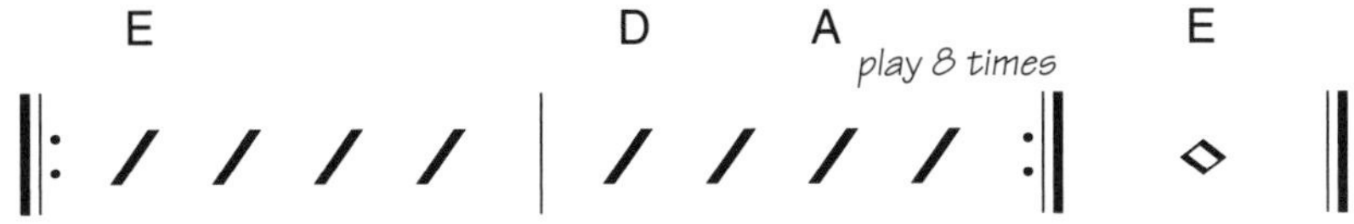

E      D    A      E

*play 8 times*

‖: / / / / | / / / / :‖ ◇ ‖

**FastTrack** is the fastest way for beginners to learn to play the instrument they just bought. **FastTrack** is different from other method books: we've made our book/audio packs user-friendly with plenty of cool songs that make it easy and fun for players to teach themselves. Plus, the last section of the books have the same songs so that students can form a band and jam together. Songbooks for guitar, bass, keyboard and drums are all compatible, and feature eight songs. All packs include great play-along audio with a professional-sounding back-up band.

# FastTrack Bass
*by Blake Neely & Jeff Schroedl*

### Level 1
| | | |
|---|---|---|
| 00264732 | Method Book/Online Media | $14.99 |
| 00697284 | Method Book/Online Audio | $7.99 |
| 00696404 | Method Book/Online Audio + DVD | $14.99 |
| 00697289 | Songbook 1/Online Audio | $12.99 |
| 00695368 | Songbook 2/Online Audio | $12.99 |
| 00696440 | Rock Songbook with CD | $12.99 |
| 00696058 | DVD | $7.99 |

### Level 2
| | | |
|---|---|---|
| 00697294 | Method Book/Online Audio | $9.99 |
| 00697298 | Songbook 1/Online Audio | $12.99 |
| 00695369 | Songbook 2/Online Audio | $12.99 |

# FastTrack Drum
*by Blake Neely & Rick Mattingly*

### Level 1
| | | |
|---|---|---|
| 00264733 | Method Book/Online Media | $14.99 |
| 00697285 | Method Book/Online Audio | $7.99 |
| 00696405 | Method Book/Online Audio + DVD | $14.99 |
| 00697290 | Songbook 1/Online Audio | $12.99 |
| 00695367 | Songbook 2/Online Audio | $12.99 |
| 00696441 | Rock Songbook with CD | $12.99 |
| 00696059 | DVD | $7.99 |

### Level 2
| | | |
|---|---|---|
| 00697295 | Method Book/Online Audio | $9.99 |
| 00697299 | Songbook 1/Online Audio | $12.99 |
| 00695371 | Songbook 2/Online Audio | $12.99 |

# FastTrack Guitar
For Electric or Acoustic Guitar, or Both
*by Blake Neely & Jeff Schroedl*

### Level 1
| | | |
|---|---|---|
| 00264731 | Method Book/Online Media | $14.99 |
| 00697282 | Method Book/Online Audio | $7.99 |
| 00696403 | Method Book/Online Audio + DVD | $14.99 |
| 00697287 | Songbook 1/Online Audio | $12.99 |
| 00695343 | Songbook 2/Online Audio | $12.99 |
| 00696438 | Rock Songbook with CD | $12.99 |
| 00696057 | DVD | $7.99 |

### Level 2
| | | |
|---|---|---|
| 00697286 | Method Book/Online Audio | $9.99 |
| 00697296 | Songbook/Online Audio | $14.99 |

### Chords & Scales
| | | |
|---|---|---|
| 00697291 | Book/Online Audio | $10.99 |

# FastTrack Keyboard
For Electric Keyboard, Synthesizer or Piano
*by Blake Neely & Gary Meisner*

### Level 1
| | | |
|---|---|---|
| 00264734 | Method Book/Online Media | $14.99 |
| 00697283 | Method Book/Online Audio | $7.99 |
| 00696406 | Method Book/Online Audio + DVD | $14.99 |
| 00697288 | Songbook 1/Online Audio | $12.99 |
| 00696439 | Rock Songbook with CD | $12.99 |
| 00696060 | DVD | $7.99 |

### Level 2
| | | |
|---|---|---|
| 00697293 | Method Book/Online Audio | $9.99 |

### Chords & Scales
| | | |
|---|---|---|
| 00697292 | Book/Online Audio | $9.99 |

# FastTrack Harmonica
*by Blake Neely & Doug Downing*

### Level 1
| | | |
|---|---|---|
| 00695407 | Method Book/Online Audio | $7.99 |
| 00695958 | Mini Method Book with CD | $7.95 |
| 00820016 | Mini Method/CD + Harmonica | $12.99 |
| 00695574 | Songbook/Online Audio | $12.99 |

### Level 2
| | | |
|---|---|---|
| 00695889 | Method Book/Online Audio | $9.99 |
| 00695891 | Songbook with CD | $12.99 |

# FastTrack Lead Singer
*by Blake Neely*

### Level 1
| | | |
|---|---|---|
| 00695408 | Method Book/Online Audio | $7.99 |
| 00695410 | Songbook/Online Audio | $14.99 |

### Level 2
| | | |
|---|---|---|
| 00695890 | Method Book/Online Audio | $9.95 |
| 00695892 | Songbook with CD | $12.95 |

# FastTrack Saxophone
*by Blake Neely*

### Level 1
| | | |
|---|---|---|
| 00695241 | Method Book/Online Audio | $7.99 |
| 00695409 | Songbook/Online Audio | $14.99 |

# FastTrack Ukulele
*by Chad Johnson*

### Level 1
| | | |
|---|---|---|
| 00114417 | Method Book/Online Audio | $7.99 |
| 00158671 | Songbook/Online Audio | $12.99 |

### Level 2
| | | |
|---|---|---|
| 00275508 | Method Book/Online Audio | $9.99 |

# FastTrack Violin
*by Patrick Clark*

### Level 1
| | | |
|---|---|---|
| 00141262 | Method Book/Online Audio | $7.99 |

**HAL•LEONARD®**

Visit Hal Leonard online at **www.halleonard.com**

*Prices, contents, and availability subject to change without notice.*
*Some products may not be available outside the U.S.A. Spanish and French editions also available.*

0920
021